HEROES
AND
MONSTERS

HANNAH KENDRICK

ISBN-13: 978-1-954609-26-6

This book was printed in the United States of America

All information is solely considered as the point of view of the author.

To order additional copies of this book contact:

LaBoo Publishing Enterprise, LLC
staff@laboopublishing.com
www.laboopublishing.com

TABLE OF CONTENTS

INTRODUCTION

Hannah sits on an overstuffed leather couch, in an elaborately decorated yet warm and inviting living room. Red is the dominant color, splashed generously across Persian rugs and a variety of tasseled, embroidered throw pillows. The furniture is heavy, carved wood, set against a backdrop of lavish brocade curtains and borders lined with sparkling garlands. The walls are lined with family portraits grouped together in artfully mismatched frames, the shelves filled with candid snapshots and mementos of a life filled with laughter and love. Hannah is happy, outspoken, and carries an attitude of fearlessness and determination. Even as she relaxes into her favorite seat in the house, there is the sense that she is not only prepared for the unexpected, but ready and able to handle it efficiently—and perhaps most significantly, without fear.

Hannah's story is astonishing, the sort of information your mind and heart simply want to reject. The depths of human cruelty and callousness that she has endured are so extreme that you will find yourself struggling to accept it, even as the undeniable evidence is displayed before you. Fire has left its indelible marks upon her skin, covering her entire upper body in a pattern of soft whirls and divots, a testimony to the suffering she has endured at the hands of her ex-husband and so many others—all of whom were meant to be heroes, but revealed themselves to be monsters. At times shocking in its violence and the lengths she had to go to in order not only to survive, but truly thrive as a mother and a woman of unshakable faith, Hannah's story is ultimately one of redemption and transformation through the power of forgiveness and unconditional love. Hers is a tale to remind us of all that we are stronger than we think, and to remind us:

In the middle of life's Great Storms, when happiness feels like a fading memory, believe that you are loved; that you do not suffer alone; and that you too can overcome and thrive.

CHAPTER ONE

My mother was born August 1, 1955, to Mr. and Mrs. Mathis in east Texas. She was the youngest of the first four out of thirteen children they put up for adoption. You see, Mr. and Mrs. Mathis divorced, and my grandparents Mr. and Mrs. Abshire adopted the youngest two, naming them Lynn Abshire and Leah Katherine Abshire. They got back together several times, having a total of thirteen children all together, eleven of which I have no clue about, but Leah Abshire is my mom. The Abshires resided in Morgan City, Louisiana, and that is where my mother grew up and attended and graduated high school. She was even a Tigerorette.

My name is Hannah Kathleen Kendrick. I was born March 11, 1981, in Osage Beach, Missouri. After she graduated at age 18, my mother felt forced to marry a man she did not actually love, the infamous Mr. Kendrick. That lasted just a few months and he was gone, and they never saw each other again as far as I know. Not long after that, my mother met my oldest sister Heather's father. In the state of Louisiana, if you are married it is the law that the child takes the father's last name, and my sister's name is Heather Kendrick. At some point they split up and she met the father of my second oldest sister, Roci. He talked her into hitchhiking to Oregon; she was pregnant and did not know it. When it was all said and done, they ended up hitchhiking to his hometown, Buffalo, Missouri. Here Momma was, with two baby girls, two deadbeat daddies, and all alone. But she was still going and doing the best she could, and she met my father Oscar Ray Nichols, aka Junior. He came from a well-respected family from Kansas City, Missouri, that moved to Buffalo, Missouri, and opened a mom-and-pop bait and tackle gas station by Bennett Springs. This is a well-known Trout Conservation area, and the family did very well there. My father's mother Margie Nichols died when my father was very young. I really don't know much about her. It was said that she had heart problems, but I also know she had many battles with mental health issues, and several times was admitted to the state hospital in Nevada, Missouri, where I would end up one day, but that's years down the road. Because of my family being who they were, a lot was hidden. No dark secrets were ever to see the light in that family, but I am going to illuminate them. He was born March 19, 1961, to Margaryann Nichols and Oscar Ray Nichols Sr. When my mother and father met, they quickly became really good friends. There was quite a group of them that would hang out and party all the time. Apparently, sometimes they would be more than friends, because at some point my father heard that my mother was pregnant. Suddenly this charming, fun friend turned into something different, as he asked her about her pregnancy with evil in his eyes. She replied, "Yes I am pregnant, but it is by a guy named Mike." He said, "It better be, because you know I would kick that bastard fucking baby right out of you." He left, and Mom went on to carry me and take care of my sisters all alone as usual, while my dad went off to Tulsa Welding School.

I was born not too many weeks after he had come back from welding school in Buffalo. Buffalo being a very small town of less than two thousand, my dad had heard through a group of friends that I was born with bright red hair. He had also been born with bright red hair, so he went straight to my momma's house. As I remember my dad telling me, he walked in and looked at me in the crib, and he saw my bright red hair, my bright blue eyes, and his daddy's ears. He never could have imagined he would love me as much as he did, and he had no choice but to make me, my mom, my sisters, and him a family. He vowed to never leave us. We had no idea how bad that was going to end up, but we would soon see.

My earliest memories are from when I was around three years old. I would wake up really early, while it was still dark outside, around four or five am, and hear Dad yelling at Mom. He would be calling her names like cunt, which was one of his favorites, and telling her she was worthless because he couldn't get out the door quick enough to work and he ought to just shoot her. My dad stockpiled guns and bullets in our house. He always had a gun on him, so I would be in my bed trying to be quiet while I was crying and praying to God, "Don't hear gun shots, don't hear gun shots, don't hear gun shots." I would pray that he would just leave and go to work. I knew from a very young age that God was who I was supposed to be praying to. Then he would leave for work, and through the day everything would be okay. I would even watch him pull in our long driveway. I would run towards him through the gate and catch him right as he was getting out of the truck, and he would pick me up. It was like that monster from that morning did not even exist anymore. It seemed like the only time dad was happy was when he was teaching us stuff about guns, fishing, or hunting.

My family and I lived on a big farm outside of Buffalo, Missouri. My momma always tended to a big garden and chickens, so we literally grew or killed everything we ate. My mom was an amazing homemaker. She made our clothes, and curtains, grew all of our vegetables, and made amazing homemade Cajun meals with all of the wild meat dad caught and killed. For fun for us, Mom would save us by packing us a big lunch after breakfast and send us out into the fields to play. We did not have to come home all day, and we had three ponds on the farm. She did this to protect us, so that if Dad was in a bad mood, we wouldn't have to see anything.

My parents used to keep a keg in the barn in the refrigerator. We were so scared to go into the house to get something cold to drink, so we would go out to the old fridge in the barn. We would drink the really cold, brisky stuff that at that age did taste nasty, but it was cold and that part was good. So I look back now with a thousand percent certainty that at three and four years old, me, my sisters, and our friends were running around on a farm drunk.

We didn't want to go inside, because the three main punishments my dad had on a whim would be to pick the carpet (he did not see any need for a vacuum, because he had three kids), hold his boots, or the merry-go-round. This last consisted of me and my two sisters standing in line, starting with Heather. He would spank her until he was done, and then move down the line to my sister Roci, and then on to me. He'd rotate us until he felt the punishment had been sufficient. My mother would be in the next room crying because there was nothing she could do for us.

My dad was exceptionally hard on my oldest sister Heather, and Heather always tried to protect me and Roci. One time I left the light on upstairs. Heather took the blame for me, and my dad kicked her all the way up the stairs with his steel-toed boots. I will never forget the cries or the bruises that he left on her back. But he had an even sicker fixation for Roci. She specifically hated mushrooms, and he knew that. He ordered pizza with mushrooms on it—it was rare for my dad to pay for food—and he forced her to eat it. As a result, she puked, and he forced her to eat that too.

Unfortunately, it gets worse. I will never forget when Roci and I were taking a bath together, which we did to conserve water. My father came into the bathroom and asked me to leave. To be honest, at that moment I felt extremely jealous, because he was my dad and I wanted to know why he wouldn't share with me what he was wanting to share with Roci. What could he possibly be doing or telling her that I could not be a part of? I was pacing back and forth, and it seemed like forever before he came out of the bathroom. I promptly asked him, "Dad, what did you do with Roci?" He replied quickly, "I was telling her to put deodorant on her stomach." Then I felt relieved, because that made sense to me: Roci was older and was supposed to be wearing deodorant, and I was four years old, so I didn't think much about it.

But dad was just extremely one way or the other. He was either extremely mean or extremely happy or extremely violent. It could change in a split second. I remember one time Momma had taken us to get a family picture, which was just her and us girls, because Dad did not want to go. We got family pictures made at Wal-Mart. Back then you had to schedule to have pictures made, because people would travel into town to do it. We went to take our pictures, and they had a blouse on clearance for two dollars. My sisters and I talked my mom into buying it, because she deserved it and had nothing nice to wear. We took the pictures, and they turned out wonderful. We proceeded to travel home to Dad, who had been frying fish for an hour or so before we got home, because the grease wasn't that hot. As soon as we walked in, the words that came out of his mouth were, "You worthless fucking cunt, where the fuck did you get that shirt? You wasted my fucking money you worthless bitch," as he threw the pan of fish fry grease on her. This made it forever humiliating for her to hang that family picture, because we knew what price she paid to wear that two-dollar baby blue blouse.

One morning in winter, Mom and Heather went into town. I was not in school yet, so I must have been four or four and a half years old. Me, Dad, and Roci were snuggled in my twin-size bed because I had the TV at the end of my bed. Dad made me go to the end of the bed while he snuggled with Roci at the top. Again, that jealous feeling came, but I was right there not knowing what I was not a part of. But it was something that didn't feel right. Being four and a half, what did I know?

Some time passed, and next thing I knew, my sisters were telling me, "Come on let's go, we are leaving." They promised they would buy me a baby doll, saying, "We are getting on a bus to go to Texas to live with Mom's friend." Mom did buy me the baby doll, and we rode the bus to Houston, Texas. We were down there roughly a month before my mom's friend contacted my dad and told him where we were. My mom had told my sister Heather that my dad knew where we were and that my mom's friend told my dad that he needed to come get us or she was going to put us out.

My sister Heather was in fear because she knew the truth: that dad had been molesting Roci and had tried molesting her. Heather told one of her friends at school, because she was scared. I did not find any of this out until later. In my eyes, all I knew was I was outside playing, and I saw what looked to be my dad's truck pulling up. I was in disbelief to see my dad. I was so excited, my evil monster hero. He got out of the truck and had a Shera doll waiting for me. It was like nothing had ever happened and we were again a happy family.

We moved back to Missouri, and he had got us a house in Long Lane, Missouri. On our first or second day of school at Long Lane Elementary, they called me and each one of my sisters into the counselor's office. The counselor and other adults were asking me about my home life, but specifically my dad. I was telling them the truth because it was normal to me. I did not know that dads did not beat their children or their moms. I did not think anything of it, because it was normal for us. That day we were riding the bus home and there was a cop behind the bus. I will never forget it, because the older kids were making fun of the bus driver telling them that they were going to get pulled over and go to jail. I was not thinking anything of it, and the bus driver stopped at the driveway, and they helped us off the bus. The police car followed us up our long driveway, so it felt like it took forever to get there. My sister took me and Roci into the bathroom and shut us in there and locked the door. As the police officer walked in, my dad was breaking up pounds of weed at the kitchen table. We stayed locked in the bathroom until the officers had arrested my father and removed him from our home. But it didn't take him long to immediately bond out, because of who my dad's family was—pillars of the community and all. The sexual molestation charges and abuse allegations were dropped immediately. But the weed charges were picked up and he did end up serving fourteen months at a state prison in Missouri. We finished out the school year in Long Lane while Mom worked at a blue jean factory in Lebanon, Missouri. But when summer came, Mom had no one to watch us girls, so she called for help from our family in Louisiana and Heather's biological grandparents, who were complete strangers to us. They all came up and got us while my mom stayed back and worked so she could save money to eventually move to Louisiana. She wanted to be far away when he got out of prison for good.

CHAPTER TWO

Now I was living in Louisiana with Heather's grandparents, in a Southern-style Victorian home with many cousins and learning all kinds of things that we never learned in the countryside of Missouri. We learned about new music we had never heard, we learned about a new culture, and had only seen white people. We learned that we were the minority, and that everyone is the same regardless of their skin color, which was the opposite of what my father felt. We were so excited for our mother to come down and live with us. I cried for her often because I missed her hugs, her smell, everything. Especially her food. It's funny how everything my momma does is perfect. Finally, she made it down there with us. Heather's grandpa gave us a trailer to live in and we put it in a trailer park. By God, we tied it to cement blocks and made it ours.

We did pretty good for a while. That was until Heather met her first real boyfriend, who I won't name. He was about fifteen and I was seven. He told me he was going to break up with my sister if I did not suck his dick. I said, "My sister really, really loves you, and you will break her heart." He said, "That won't happen if you just suck my dick." I responded with, "Okay I will, because I don't want you to break her heart." I remembered me leaving the light on and what dad did to her, so I felt like I owed it to her. I began to try. I told him it tasted really nasty, and at that time I remembered a popular song by Def Leppard, which was "Pour Some Sugar on Me." I put the sugar on his dick and even put some in my mouth and proceeded to do it. I don't really remember how it went, but I do remember that he still broke up with my sister and I ended up telling her what happened. I felt disgusted and ashamed for what I did. I realized later that what he did was sexual molestation.

Louisiana became really expensive for my mom. She had to work two and three jobs and was still barely making it. The cost of living in Missouri was so much cheaper and healthier, so she decided it would be best to save up some money and move us back up here. We moved back to Buffalo where we stayed with a close friend of hers until we got our own place. It was awesome, because we were right in town, this time on Main Street. There was an apartment complex two blocks from my house filled with kids of all ages for me and my sisters to play with. At this point I had started my third-grade year and I had met my best friends Tori, Gina, Christina, Twila, and LaDonna. LaDonna is the only one that I did not meet at church, because she lived at the apartment complex. In Buffalo, as a kid, there's nothing to do besides go to church. On Tuesdays and Thursdays, we would go to the Pentecostal church and on Wednesdays and Sundays we would go to the Baptist church. And I'm not sure when, but we made it to the Assembly of God church as well, and we also made it to all Baptist Bible School classes. I was baptized in all three churches.

When I was a little girl on the farm, my favorite thing to do was catch tadpoles, crawdads, eat sour grass and catch lighting bugs. It was always a treat when Momma and Daddy would take us to the drive-in movie theater, so it was a huge surprise when Dad said he and Momma were going into town to get us a movie. I was so excited! After all we lived on a huge farm, so I remember looking around our yard wondering where Dad was going to put that big, huge screen. Of course, he and Momma came in with a VCR they had rented from our local grocery store. I didn't even know such a thing existed.

When Momma got to Louisiana with us life really changed, No more violence in our home. Lots of laughs and smiles. We didn't have much, and Momma worked a lot, but we had a lot of fun. Me and my sisters and Mom were free to buy what we wanted, but most importantly we didn't have to do anything we didn't want to. Momma would wear makeup. She would have friends and my uncles over for cards and would have seafood boils and music. We always had music going. Just good family fun for the most part. My love for exploring definitely had not changed, just the climate. You can find some really fun stuff in the swamps. I could still find crawdads, but here they were called crawfish. My favorite was salamanders. I came a little too close to a gator a time or two. I would say I should have been more careful, but fear just was not in me when it comes to nature and animals, and it still isn't. I love both still to this day. Rainy days are my favorite. I came close to making friends with a rabid racoon in my twenties.

So some of the things that started happening in Louisiana, without real rules and Momma always working and my sisters in charge, were drinking and smoking cigarettes. One time I remember my sisters bribing me to stay outside and play and leave them alone. They said they would give me a cigarette, and I took the bribe, but did not keep my word. I snuck in to see what they were doing, and they were all watching what I would find out later was called porno. I was seven years old. I remember it was 1988 and back then there was no age limit on tobacco sales. I remember getting a dollar from my momma to get, of all things, cough drops and, on my way to school, I stopped at the local mom and pop store and bought my first pack of pyramid cigarettes for seventy-two cents. Later that evening my momma was having one of her get togethers and my uncle caught me red handed smoking in my closet. For the first time ever, Momma said I was going to get an ass whooping and to get my ass in there. So I did what I had to do. I put on every pair of pants

I owned and went to face Momma. You can just about guess what happened next. She made me get bare ass naked and I got three or four appropriate swats on my butt, not abuse in my eyes. I know because I remember screaming at her that she was abusive for doing that to me like Dad. The next day she came home with a bunch of real information and articles and even a movie of real stories about abuse, and I realized what Momma did was not abuse—that there was a difference, a huge difference.

But things in Louisiana were definitely different. The culture, I loved. My neighbors were a family of seven with five kids from age two to fifteen and we had so much fun. I had never seen or met a black person, an Asian, or anyone except a white person. A little country girl growing up on a farm whose best friend was a frog or a cow, this was huge. I definitely took an ass whooping when I met my first best friend that was black, because I asked her why she was black. We became very close after that. I had no idea then, but I understood why it was rude after. She also understood when I told her where I was from.

So Momma pretty much trusted us girls to do the right thing. Boy was she wrong. She used to take my oldest sister to work with her sometimes, leaving Roci in charge. Heather was six years older than me, and Roci was four years older than me, so they were thirteen and eleven at the time. Heather and her best friend went to work with Momma to her overnight job. It was a gas station convenience store. They were there to keep Momma company and help Momma stock shelves, and boy did they. They stole one of each bottle of alcohol from the store.

We used to go to the local skating rink every weekend, and every other weekend they would have a lock-in. It was from 6pm to 6am. My sister and her best friend smuggled all the alcohol in, and I don't recall them getting caught. I just will never forget they did that. I had the best times at the lock-ins. At midnight they would have lip-synching contests, and one time I actually won first place! IT WAS SO COOL!! My sisters and everyone were cheering me on. The whole crowd was holding up lit lighters. I was lip-synching "You're all I Need" by Motley Crew. It was the best feeling ever at that age. I think I won $100 and some kind of trophy. But most importantly I felt talented and special. It wasn't long after that we moved back to Missouri, and I would miss everything about my Cajun roots.

Ladonna was my very special friend. She lived in the apartment complex, so I was able to see her the most. She also stayed at my house most often, but sometimes I was able to stay at hers. When she would stay at mine, we would watch the movie *Beaches* over and over and over again. She was Hilary and I was Cecilia Bloom. One particular night I happened to be staying at LaDonna's house and her parents were drinking. I had never paid much attention to her stepdad; he was pretty much a lump that laid on the couch under a blanket while her mother worked at a steakhouse. That particular night, LaDonna had an army cot in her room, and at the last minute she was saying how she wanted to sleep in her parents' bed because we could not fit on the cot together comfortably, but we could. Her stepdad replied, "No, because me and your mom are going to have sex tonight. We will come and get you when we are done." I thought that to be extremely odd, and unlike anything I had ever experienced, and I had experienced some bizarre things in my eight years of life.

We went to bed later, and I was wone up by her stepdad standing on my side of the cot butt naked, and my tight biker shorts had been pulled down to my knees. At first, coming up out of a dead sleep, I was confused, because I sometimes took my clothes off while I was asleep because I would get uncomfortable. But at that time, I also knew that LaDonna was supposed to be going to lay in their bed. Within five seconds of waking up out of a dead sleep to a naked man who was supposed to be coming to get LaDonna to go and sleep in their bed, he said real nonchalantly, "No, no," and just walked out of the room. I was in such a daze I just pulled my biker shorts back up and was confused. It kind of felt like I was in a dream state, and I fell back asleep. Later, I again awoke abruptly, and felt his fingers pressing against my vagina. Except this time, he was on all fours at the end of the bed, and I could not see him, I could just feel his fingers grabbing and touching my vagina. I knew what was going on in that moment because I was fully awake. I started moving my legs, at first slowly because I was scared, but then I moved my legs back and forth faster, making it even harder for him to touch me. It worked. He crawled out of the room, still naked. I attempted to awaken LaDonna briefly, but I really just wanted my mom.

I have no idea what time it was, I just remember it being dark outside. I slowly got on my shoes and was quiet as a church mouse until I got the door closed. As soon as I got outside, I ran like hell to my momma, and banged on her window crying to let me in the house. The safest place I have ever been in my entire life is laying my head on my mom's chest with her arms wrapped around me. No matter how old I am, there has never been a safer place. The next day we went and reported what had happened, and the police arrested him. But the worst part was her mother did not believe any of it, and her mother chose him over LaDonna, and she was taken into DFS custody. I did not see her again until we went to court a year and a half later. When we went to court, I did exactly what I was supposed to do. I got on the stand and told the truth. Whenever the closing argument came, his defense attorney argued that I had put my father in prison for allegations of child molestation against me and got rid of my dad successfully, and that LaDonna's stepdad and mom did not like me being friends with her. Since they did not want us to be friends, I made all of this up to get rid of him so we could continue to be friends. They said that, because I showed no emotion on the stand, I must have been making all of it up. My answer to that was, "Why should I cry when I did not do anything wrong?" I knew he was guilty and God knew he was guilty. They thought that I did not show enough emotion. Well, I showed a lot of emotion when they read out the verdict of "Not Guilty." In that moment it felt like I had lost my mind. How could God let this man get away with this? I walked down the courthouse steps screaming and crying inconsolably, while he and his buddies were high fiving about his victory over getting away with touching a nine-year-old child.

Chapter Three

In 1992 I was about eleven and a half and my mom and my mom's boyfriend belonged to an Amvet's social club for American veterans. They were doing their annual picnic at Stockton Lake, Missouri. It was an all-weekend picnic and a campout, which was fun for the whole family. I was in charge of giving out sodas for free for all the children and non-alcohol drinkers because it was a free social event for vets. It was donation only. I was standing at my booth handing out sodas when lo and behold who walked up to my booth to get a soda? LaDonna's ex stepdad, who had molested me and got away with it, and a female companion with long dark hair that I had never seen before. He had a smile on his face while he was trying to ask me for a soda. I took off to find my mom, running and crying. I couldn't believe he was there. How dare he be so arrogant, narcissistic, and torturous? He was just a predator. I cried and cried to my mom, and she assured me that they would make him leave and that we weren't going anywhere. He did, I guess, because I did not see him the rest of the weekend. About two years later, when I was thirteen years old, I was playing outside my friend Twila's house in Buffalo, and that mysterious lady with the long dark hair drove by and recognized me. She stopped and said, "I know what he did to you, I believe you." I asked her how she knew, and she said, "Because I walked in on him doing it to my three-year-old daughter. He is in prison now." Ron Mowery is now a registered sex offender and has been back to prison multiple times for the same offense.

In the midst of all of this, my mom had actually run into my father's wife Kitty. My mom was at Amvets Bar enjoying herself with her boyfriend when a lady approached her. She said she was married to my father and wanted to know if she could have a heart-to-heart woman talk with my mom. My mom said, "Of course." I believe they shut the bar down and brought their conversation to the house, because my mom brought her home and introduced her as my dad's wife. I got excited, because I had not seen my dad in a long time and I wanted to see my him, even though I knew he had molested my sister and everything he had done. Within an hour, even in the middle of the night, after my mom gave Kitty the okay, my dad was in my driveway. Just like the three-year-old girl I once was, I was running right into my evil monster hero's arms again. My mom allowed me to even leave with him that night, and I remember the next day that Kitty vowed to protect me, and Mom knew that dad would never hurt me. He was really hard on my sisters, but because I was the baby, he always took it easier on me. When we would get punished, my sisters would get a twenty beating on a scale from one to ten, and I would get a one.

So, I was able to go home with my dad that night, and I remember he took me to Walmart that next day and told me I could get anything and everything I wanted. I picked out a Barbie dream house, new Barbie dolls, and a new bicycle. I had never had anything like that. I even got lots of new clothes. I felt like a princess. He was so happy that whole visit, I thought my dad had actually changed. So I stayed the night again, and it was that next morning that I heard those familiar sounds. It seemed as though Kitty had the same name as my mom, which was "You worthless fucking cunt." It would be so insane, because he would be beating her and telling her how she did not even deserve to live but would be smiling at me and winking at me with approval of love for me. I was just ready to go home. I didn't care about the material things he got me; I was just ready to go home to my mom.

Needless to say, I still kept a visiting relationship with my dad, but I only visited about every two months overnight. The max I ever stayed with him after that was two nights. One time, we were going to Springfield to get Kitty's eyeglasses that she needed from Sears. While we were there they had women's holiday sweaters on sale. Dad was pointing out how pretty they would look on Kitty. She was saying, "Oh no Junior, I don't need another sweater." He was rubbing her shoulders, hugging on her, and kissing on her telling her she deserved it because she was such a hardworking waitress. They made a lot of money, and he was a hardworking truck driver that did not pay child support at that time. Dad insisted that Kitty pick out a holiday sweater. She did, and we got her glasses and headed back to Buffalo. We were about five miles outside of Springfield, heading towards Buffalo, and out of nowhere Dad flipped out and said, "All you do is just waste our fucking money. I got to spend money on your fucking glasses, your sweater, I just need to fucking get rid of you. Matter of fact, I will do it right now." We were in a standard S10 pickup truck. Dad was driving, I was in the middle, and Kitty was next to me. Dad was very big: he was 6'4 and had long arms and long legs. He reached over and opened her passenger door while we were driving 65 to 70 miles per hour down the highway and started pushing her out of the truck. I was holding onto her, so if she went out, I was going with her. Kitty got the door back shut and everybody in the truck went completely silent. Before we knew it, we were in Buffalo. Dad pipes up, saying that he needed to feed his ladies. He proceeded to ask us if we wanted to go to the steakhouse, because it was the least he could do. It wasn't a question, it was an order to fix your face, get your shit together, and act like we were a happy family. But Kitty and I both knew what had really happened on the way there. We just knew better than to do anything other than what he expected of us.

I think it was about my next visit with my dad a couple months later that I had suggested to Kitty that she really needed to leave my dad and that she could stay with me and my mom. I knew that my mom would not mind it. I was sick and tired of seeing her get beaten by my dad on my visits, and I also told her that I understood if she ever had to kill my dad to protect herself. In the middle of the night, she packed up what she could. I found out later it was a couple pounds of weed and just a few clothes. She made sure to get me and my stuff, and we went to my mom's. That lasted about three days. We did not even have a phone, and all my dad had to do was pull in my driveway and honk one time, and she went back to him. But of course she made sure to leave my mom with some weed.

This whole time my mom had been trying to get my dad for child support. But because my dad was from the family he was from, the pillars of the community, child support papers had a way of never being filed all the way through in Dallas County. When I was thirteen, we moved to Springfield, and the case was switched to Greene County. My dad was then finally served child support papers, and he was pissed! A lot of things changed. For one, Kitty completely turned on me, and started making up lies about me to my dad. I can only think that she was getting extra abuse because they could not convince me to live with them, which would be the only way to stop the child support order. At that time my sister Roci had also became pregnant and had my oldest nephew. She was sixteen when she got pregnant and seventeen when she gave birth. My oldest sister Heather also became pregnant, and Dylan was born six months after Alex. I was so excited to be an aunt since I had been the baby my whole life. I loved them so much.

But I still had to battle my dad and my stepmom, who were trying to bribe me with everything to get me to go live with them: from a brand-new car when I turned 16, to basically saying I could have anything I wanted as long as I went to go live with them. Finally, I had to do the hardest thing ever had to do in my life thus far, and that was to tell my dad the truth to his face. "Dad I cannot live with you," I screamed at him with all of might. "You are a child molester. I remember you putting guns to my mom's head, I remember you beating my mom, and I watched you beat Kitty every fucking day. I only come and visit you every other month because you are happy for at least one day and not beating up Kitty. I have to make my visits short because you are fucking insane, violent, and crazy. I love you, but I will never fucking live with you. You are a child molester, and I know what the fuck you did to Roci because I was there in the bed when it happened. When you made me leave the bathroom and told me the story about the deodorant, I was young then, but I'm not fucking young now. I know what you did, and I will never fucking live with you. I don't give a fuck what you could give me. You can't even address your mental illness or admit you need help." My father respected my wishes and our relationship went on accordingly.

Chapter Four

I was thirteen and I had nephews. I had never been more excited because, like I said, I was the baby of the family with no cousins, because my dad was an only child and didn't know any of my mom's biological family. Throughout my childhood I would be told I was just like my dad in so many ways by my sisters and mother. It could be something as simple as the way that I walked, or the fact that I was mean and easily aggressive, or that I never backed down from a challenge. I never liked being told I was just like my dad, because I never wanted to be like him, and I already looked just like him. In a family full of brunettes with olive skin, I am the pale redhead with blue eyes. It took me thirty-eight years to repeat this out loud, but I can say it now with full confidence without being ashamed or embarrassed: because I had been told I was just like my dad in so many ways, when my nephews were first born, I felt so much joy and happiness, but then I felt impending doom, because deep in my heart I actually believed that I was just like my dad, because I did feel violent and angry a lot.

That meant that if I felt those things like him, that one day something might click and I might be attracted to children. I concluded that it would be best for me to kill myself, and quick, before I hurt one of the nephews that I really loved. I felt like a ticking time bomb and was waiting to wake up one day and have an overwhelming attraction to children. Because after all, I was just like my dad, right? So I swallowed my first bottle of pills and ended up in Lakeland Regional Hospital at the age of thirteen. The only thing I would tell anyone is that I didn't want to live. I never told them the truth, I just said that the world was dark, and I didn't want to be here anymore. In the next two years, till I was fifteen and a half, I was hospitalized five times. Three of those were in Lakeland and the other two were at the Marion Center.

After I got out at fifteen and a half, I had hooked up with some friends that I had met at the school for kids with behavioral problems called Excel. We actually all met at the city bus station waiting to catch the bus to Excel. We would all bring whatever we could—weed, cigarettes, alcohol, lighters—and we would get fucked up before we went to school. That became an everyday thing for me. I met people that would become my life-long friends that I am still friends with today: Orlando, DJ, Amanda V., Marlon, Catherine, Jamie, Rose, Gerdy, Tisha, Antonio and Tim Draper, and Derek T. We were always together and an extremely tight crew of friends that would do anything for each other. We started going to clubs when we were fifteen, just me and the girls.

When I was around fifteen years old my sister Heather gave birth to my beautiful niece Sebrina Ingram. I was able to get a job with a fake ID at Burger King. I got us all an apartment for Heather, my nephew Dylan, Sebrina, Amanda V and I. The landlord did not check any of my information. We were in! Not long after that I met a man, we will call him Bobby. I was still 15 years old at the time, he took a liking to me, but Bobby sold crack and was 23. I met him at a party in 1997, and he gave me the keys to his 1996 Berratta on triple gold Dayton's with a car phone and a 100-dollar bill. I had never met anyone like him before, a black man with a mouth full of gold teeth. I was smitten. He told me he had some business to take care of but he wanted to make sure he could see me later, so he gave me his car and he would call me on his car phone to tell me where to meet him when he was done handling his business. It was already apparent to me that he was dealing crack, and I was like, "What's up?" I knew he had the money, and I did not have anything else to do.

I was young, and I did not want to have anything to do with what my dad raised me to believe, so I went the complete opposite. One day my dad saw that I was smoking Newport menthols and said that the only thing I could do to cause him to turn his back on me for was to sleep outside of my race. He believed that sleeping outside of your race is like a deer and turkey fucking. Obviously, my cigarettes made him feel some type of way. The second worst thing that could happen was ending up with a bunch of bastard babies that I could not take care of living on Commercial Street. That happened later on in the future, except my babies are not bastards.

Me and Bobby's relationship progressed, and I had started the routine of riding around with him while he was selling crack. Me and Bobby dated until Bobby got caught up selling crack and went to prison at Algoa Penitentiary in Missouri. After I turned 16, I started working at various sales jobs, which I was extremely good at. One was Savage Tech, where we sold TriStar vacuums. Then I went on to work for Culligan Water Company for four years. In July of 2000 I was 19 years old, and Bobby got out of prison. We had kept in constant contact, and I had even visited him a couple of times. We had made plans to get married and have a daughter. When he got out, he planned to go to St. Louis, to live with his grandmother. Me and my mom went up there to stay a week in a hotel room to spend time with him. When I came back to Springfield, I started hearing rumors within my circle of friends that a girl that a friend of mine knew was with the same Bobby I was with. They knew way too many details for it to be a coincidence. I found out where the girl lived and went over there and confronted her about the situation with Bobby. She said that the rumors were true, and that she knew about me. She had received one of my letters by mistake. He would duplicate letters, and one time he put my letter in her envelope. So I completely broke it

off and it was over between us. At that point I was completely crushed, and he made me feel extremely stupid.

My good friend Antonio Draper would come over
and hangout with me, while we smoked blunts and talked. Talking led to more, and by the end of August we
were friends with benefits. We were living Bob Seger's
Night Moves. We refused to tell anyone that we were
actually together but, in all actuality, we were falling
deeply in love. We ended up moving in together in
October 2000 right next door to my mom's house in
Springfield. Everything was going amazing; we were so
much in love. We were playing marathon rounds of mo-
nopoly. I was making big, huge breakfasts and dinners
for all of our friends. We would blast music and clean
together. We were young, happy, wild, free, and in love.

That changed on the morning of December 7, 2000.
He came home with his two-year-old daughter, telling
me he had stayed the night at his child's mother's house
and that he had cheated on me with her. Bobby had been
trying to contact me and was currently in Springfield and
off of house arrest. I had Bobby come and pick me up on
a rebound, and when I came back home Antonio was
still there. I will never forget because there were 21 inches of snow on the ground. I asked Antonio, "Why the
fuck are you here? We are not together, and you fucked
your baby momma. And I fucked Bobby last night. Get
out of my house now." My dad had just died a month pri-
or, in November of 2000, so I was an emotional wreck. I
even gave meth a try and did not like it, thank God.

CHAPTER FIVE

So not much changed in our family with Momma and my sisters as far as how we lived. Momma made our clothes and decorations, which often was the same material. I hated it then, I cherish it now. Momma did what she could raising three girls alone with no help from any of our dads. No help at all except of course the times when I would start seeing my dad and he would buy my clothes. My dad had never stopped growing and selling pot. As a matter a fact, he kept it drying on hangers in his closet, and every visit I would pinch some ends of the buds off and put it in my book bag to take home to my momma. I knew a few things about pot: that it was illegal, that my dad grew it and always had it, and that it made Momma laugh, and I loved when she was happy and I liked the smell, but it wasn't for little kids it was for adults, and it made the house smell good. I felt my dad owed my mom and if he wasn't going to help her or do anything then I would. I really never thought about getting caught and I never did. The real question is how at 9 years old my momma asked no questions as I was bringing her what I know now was large amounts of dad's crop.

It goes without saying that it hurt my sisters to see me have visits with my dad. I completely understood what he had done in detail at that age, and I felt guilty for still loving such a monster who had hurt my sisters and my momma so intensely, but to me he had a soft side. But only for me. He would give me this look like I was so perfect. He was also very intelligent when it came to survival skills and teaching me about the world and driving and drugs. Dad was extremely firm when he spoke, and he meant what he said as an example. Him teaching me about drugs at age eleven went like this. As he is rolling a joint, he said, "Hannah, you see this?" "Yes Dad." "This ok! EVERYTHING ELSE WILL FUCKING KILL YOU! YOU GOT THAT?" "Yes Dad, I understand!" Driving lessons went like this: "Hannah this vehicle is MORE FUCKING DANGEROUS THAN ANY GUN! IF YOU GET BEHIND THIS WHEEL YOU ARE RESPONSIBLE FOR EVERY LIFE ON THE ROAD. IF YOU ACT STUPID AND DON'T PAY ATTENTION AT ALL TIMES YOU WILL FUCKING KILL PEOPLE!! HANNAH, INNOCENT PEOPLE WILL DIE BECAUSE YOU'RE FUCKING IGNORANT! SO ALWAYS FUCKING PAY ATTENENTION BECAUSE ALOT OF THESE IGNORANT BASTARDS ARE NOT, THEY'RE FUCKING IDIOTS OUT HERE HANNAH!" "YES DADDY, I UNDERSTAND!" You may not think so, but it all stuck with me.

I'm a recovering alcoholic and yes, I abused medications doctors prescribed, but I could always hear my dad's voice when it came to hard street drugs other than pot. I tried meth but I thank God every day I didn't like it at all, not one of the maybe five times I tried. Hey, I never said I was perfect, and I hit real bottoms in my life. It's going to get way worse before it gets better, so Dad did have some positives in my life. I love to fish and I'm a damn safe driver. I actually told my children kinda the same thing about being a responsible driver, definitely not as harsh.

So my life at age eight and nine consisted of hanging out with my best friends at church. It was me, Twila, Tori, Christina and Gina. Gina and Christina were sisters. Christina was a year or so older than Gina. Their mom Miss Beverly would let us all hang out and play. So would Twila's mom, Inez was her name. Inez would become a huge part of my life, heart and family. Tori's mom was Ms. Nancy. Going to her house came with chores and babysitting her mean little brothers, and Tori stayed grounded, so if we wanted to see her it was clean the house and make sure the little monsters didn't kill each other.

Me and my friends knew we were going to be fly girls, just like the ones on *In Living Color*, the TV show. We loved rap music! Twila, Christina and Gina were all half black and white in a small white racist town in Buffalo. It was really bad. The mean kids at school would be mean to Twila a lot. Sometimes even me because she would make up embarrassing lies that everyone knew were not true. She even said that she missed school to go to the Vanilla Ice concert. She wore a very homemade jacket with bright sloppy puff paint. I honestly felt bad for her. She said Michael Jackson was her dad all the time. She had no idea how to do her hair it wouldn't seem to grow no matter what her mom, Inez would do, and Twila would always act out on her mom. This often made the babysitters quit. Twila was a huge handful and it got worse the older she got we got closer and her battle with mental illness overcame her. But back then we were always excited about the newest dance moves and hip hop beatbox music. We were into Snoop, Eazy-E, Escape, Queen Latifa, 2 Live Crew, Short Dog. We listened to hard core rap and R&B. I also loved country and rock and roll music, my friends did too.

Christina and Gina's family moved to the country just outside of Buffalo. Me and Gina went exploring as we often did out there. We crossed a fence and a creek—might I add Gina has asthma—and we were walking through the woods, and we came across an open field with a herd of cows. We wanted to see them run so I threw a rock and it actually hit a cow right in between the eyes! Me and Gina were in complete shock! The cows started running straight at us full speed. We both ran so fast back though the creek and jumped that fence. Those cows were not playing! The only thing that stopped them was the fence! I had to run and get Gina's inhaler. I never messed with a cow again. You definitely weren't going to catch me cow tipping at night.

Momma was working at the chicken plant in Buffalo for a few years there in Buffalo until she had carpal tunnel surgery. I remember the years she worked there she wore the same jeans to work every day. I never understood that, because we had thrift stores and Momma would hustle extra money by making kids clothes for her friends' kids, which they loved because it was either Walmart or thrift store or yard sales in Buffalo. Back then I think the population was under 2,000. In a small town anything different was special. Momma could make anything: food, clothes, crafts. She loved sewing and making crafts, especially for the holidays. Christmas was amazing at our house. As soon as November 1st hit we got out the Christmas trees and what decorations we had already, then spent till Christmas Eve making new ones. Our house was warm, fun, and so cozy and full of love. Momma would always make sure she read the TV guide for the Christmas movies to watch together. She tried her best to make me believe in Santa forever.

Momma had lots of friends that were really nice that just adored her Cajun cooking and her fun-loving nature. Momma would have her friends over for drinking parties all the time after the bar let out. It was not unusual to hear Garth Brooks blaring at 2am and hearing laughter and waking up to a party even on a school night. Momma also went to bars a lot, and when my sisters had plans and I did not, or if I just wanted to, Momma would take me with her and I would drink Shirley Temples and play the jukebox and line dance and listen to the adults talk about adult stuff. I could always tell when Momma had too much to drink because she would start talking about how much she loves her girls and was proud of us, and she would cry while smiling with her blue eyeshadow and red lipstick. Momma had her way of having good friends, women and men. I couldn't tell you how many aunts and uncles I claim and that claim me. Momma made mistakes, but my momma did the best she could, and I am very proud of her.

Momma met a man called Mark Charlton. He is now deceased. He became her boyfriend I believe in 1992 or 1993. He was a very gentle calm man. He was a part of Amvets social club along with his father Ernie. Amvets became a big part of our life, as did Mark an Ernie too. Mark would be a great addition and a father figure that none of us girls had ever had. He was kind and always willing to put up with our bratty bullshit, and he seemed to love Momma and all of us. He moved us all to Springfield, MO, so he could finish college.

CHAPTER SIX

I was twelve fixing to turn thirteen, and it was February 1994. Alex, my oldest nephew, Roci's son, had just been born on February 10, 1994. I had been to Springfield, MO, quite a few times, but to me it might as well have been Chicago. It seemed so huge! You have to know I had lived in the country outside Buffalo, a small town, Morgan City in Louisiana, and in Buffalo and also Long Lane, and I was so young in Houston I had no idea where I was. Springfield with half million people was uncomfortable, and worst of all, I missed Twila, Gina, Christina and Tori, but Christina and Gina's dad lived in Springfield so I would see them sometimes, but I was closest with Twila. Me and Twila were together non-stop. Either I was at her house, or she was at mine. I was at her house on a weekend hanging out at the pool hall in Buffalo when my dad caught me, and that's when I blew up and told him the truth about why I would never live with him. I remember Inez always had the words to calm me and make me feel better. We would spend hours talking to her, usually after pulling some stupid shit on her. I will never forget one of our most epic decisions to sneak out. I came up with the best idea. See, me and Twila fought like sisters sometimes, that's just how it was, and we would get over it within minutes to hours usually. Our favorite boys to hang out with lived on the same street as Twila, and we were going to surprise them and hang out with them, so I opened the window and threw my shoe out. Me and Twila went out the front door as quiet as possible, but that way if we woke up Inez I was just going to say Twila threw my shoe out and I was scared to go get it by myself so she went with me. Sounds good right? Hmmm... we got out of the house just fine. We snuck up on the boys, peeked in the window (we were too scared to knock on door) and oh gosh, the one I liked, that I had been kissing earlier, was picking his nose—ew! I was grossed out so we decided to just go back home. That was the easy part because we would be coming back in with the shoe, right? We got close enough to the house, and guess who we saw smoking a cigarette on the porch at 2am when she had to be up at 4am to go to work? We were in big trouble. She didn't make me leave but I got the same punishment as Twila. I'm still sorry to this day for causing Inez so much grief! That woman is a rock. I have seen her get up and go to work till 6pm, come home, cook, mow the yard, help with schoolwork, give baths, help her youngest with his health problems and still have time for me, a bonus problem child. She has come to my rescue many times you will see.

I started 7th grade in Springfield. I hated everything about those city kids. They made fun of me, my clothes, everything, and I was never one to back down from a fight at all. After all I was my dad's daughter and I hadn't said it yet but even at thirteen I was known for starting and finishing fights, usually with the rich popular girls or boys, it didn't matter. I was a very angry girl and happy privileged people pissed me off. If you didn't have to struggle in life, or at least respect that people do literally struggle, then there was a pretty good chance we were not going to get along. At that point I had zero respect for the justice system after what happened with my dad and with LaDonna, whom I had not seen since that horrible day in the courtroom when I was in fifth grade. She was in a foster home last I knew because our friend Amanda B, her aunt was the foster mom. But LaDonna's mom hadn't left her stepdad, but since he did end up actually getting caught later and going to prison, it would be many years before I would find LaDonna.

In Springfield I made friends with a boy named DJ. He had five sisters, but it was him that became my buddy, he and his sister Sara. DJ actually surprised me on my thirteenth birthday with Hardee's breakfast, a sausage egg and cheese Croissanwich and hash rounds and juice. He was a good friend and still is. So then I had my friend DJ and not long after, I made friends with a girl. She was new to Springfield, like me and DJ's family, and we all started hanging out. By this time, I was already smoking cigarettes daily, and pot, with my mom and sisters. Twila around that time went missing and I was trying to help Inez find her. It was about a week later she popped up with her head shaved saying she had been with skinheads down in the acid tunnels (the tunnels that go under Springfield). Inez was beside herself, heartbroken. I went with her to take Twila for inpatient treatment. It was extremely heartbreaking. Twila grabbed the pen Inez needed to sign the paperwork and tried to stab herself and staff and her mom. She was completely out of control. When we left, me and Inez just hugged each other in the car and cried for what seemed like forever.

Me, DJ, his sister Sara and our friend Mindi started going to what was called the AA dance. All we knew was it was all ages all night and I think a $1 to get in, so we would steal our parents' alcohol, whoever could get what, or have my sisters buy it in exchange for babysitting, which I did often. I had not had my breakdown just yet, but we would get drunk and go dance all night. There were a couple all night clubs that let any age in as long as you weren't trying to drink and hey, my mom trusted me. We used to go out all the time. It was not long till we met an older guy. He already had a girlfriend that Twila actually knew and he was more than willing to let us girls and even DJ come hang out at his house anytime we wanted. He would even stock his fridge full of 40oz bottles of Old English beer. His name was Big Larry. Him and his girlfriend Abby were really nice. There was nothing creepy about him, he was just a lonely guy I guess, at least that was my experience.

I only had eyes for Jeremy Houston from Buffalo. I was good friends with his sister and one of the many times I spent the night with him I decided to give up my virginity. Jeremy told me he loved me. I believed him and I was so in love with him. He had the most amazing green eyes and golden blondish brown kind of curly wild hair, with dark tan skin. HE WAS SO HOT! He had a six pack, and everything about the way he talked to me made me smile inside and out. So I let him go all the way. I did not hate it, but I would say I was not excited to do it again. It hurt—it hurt bad! The next day I went to the local swimming pool, and I caught him making out with a girl that was supposed to be one of my friends. I cried so hard! It completely broke my heart. I went back to Springfield and stopped spending so much time in Buffalo.

By this time, I was about thirteen and a half and I was clubbing on weekends and weekdays even at the Chronic Boom where I was meeting all kinds of people in that huge city. I hated school. I barely went, just enough to keep my momma off my back. I was spending all my time sad and thinking bad thoughts and thinking about how much I was just like my dad. I was helping my sister Roci constantly with my nephew Alex. I thought, while listening to "Runaway Train," I should hang myself. Then I thought *No, no I don't want my momma to find me like that, so I will just take some pills.* So I did. I got them from the medicine cabinet. I don't remember what they were, but I did end up telling my momma and she took me to the ER where they made me drink this charcoal thick nasty shit in a Styrofoam cup. You would think that would have been my last attempt but nope. I stayed in Lakeland regional for 30 days and was diagnosed with manic depression and put on 1100mg of Lithium. When I got home, I immediately quit my meds. I was right back to doing what I wanted, and that went on and off until I was fifteen, in and out of the hospitals.

One time in Marian Center, the last time as a youth (because I would return as an adult also) I actually called my dad and begged him to come in and be seen for family therapy and see a doctor also, so we could both get help. If we could both get help then we could 'fix the family history of mental illness' because at that point, I had heard many stories from my momma about my grandmother Marjory. She was abusive and suffered a mental illness and stayed at the state hospital. I never quite bought the story about heart problems, at her young age. I wanted my dad to help me save me and my future kids if I was going to have them. My dad hung up on me. I cried and cried. I felt at a complete loss and was refusing meds. I wanted to learn coping skills without drugs. Or at least I thought. I didn't consider alcohol a drug, well it is!

One day I just quit school and went to a place that only asked your SSN# and printed you an ID. So I got a job at Burger King. At this time, I was dating Bobby, my crack dealing, big balling, gold teeth, mister big money. He loved to spoil me and my whole family. He was always buying my nephews Alex and Dylan stuff. My oldest sister was pregnant and broken up with her children's father. They were on drugs and my sister was done with that life, at least she was then. Bobby was soon arrested, and I went to every court date until they sent him to prison to serve his backup from a previous case he was out on parole for. I stayed in contact, but I was fifteen, and he was twenty-three. I wasn't going to just be tied all the way down, so we stayed in touch, and I did my thing.

At this time, we were all scrunched into my momma and Mark's two-bedroom house, seven of us and Heather was due any day. So I took all my money from working and found us a duplex to live in and the landlord didn't check anything, just took my cash and let me get utilities. It was nice! It was maybe the next day or so, Sebrina Dayne Ingram was born. When we brought her home, Momma and all of us pulled together and had a crib set up in her room. It was perfect.

Not long after having Sebrina, Heather started getting high on meth again and was leaving Sebrina and Dylan with Aunt Trish, and we were just nonstop partying at the duplex. Sebrina started getting sick and Aunt Trish had to take her to the ER and they needed either Heather or Charlie, but neither could be found. They ended up putting Sebrina on a sleep apnea monitor. Heather mostly stayed at my momma's or a new boyfriend's house, so we just continued to party. It wasn't long before some of my friends, Eric, and Orlando's family came down. I really liked his cousin Jason. It was me, Amanda, Gerdy, Eric, Laura, little P and Blitz. We were a rough crew. We had each other's back, back then. We would steal cars, mostly Chrysler Lebaron convertibles. I remember we had a green racing Beretta for over a month. Every day we would wipe all our prints down and park it in an alley. Every day we would wake up without a ride and go get it again. We even put new tires on it, we probably stole them too. Basically, we were badass knuckleheads with no respect for anyone. I was completely miserable and none of my suicide attempts worked, and I didn't like happy people. I can't tell you how many times I got us kicked out the club, or we had to leave early because I punched someone. To this day I have no violent crimes on my record. Well God, me, my victims, and now you, definitely know I should.

CHAPTER SEVEN

Orlando started making trips with his cousin Jason, who I was no longer seeing intimately because he didn't want a 'girlfriend', so I moved on. I was still writing Bobby but keeping it real. I had stopped working and had taken on the family business of selling pot. I was doing what I wanted when I wanted. I even tried crystal meth that the guys brought back from Colorado.

Sebrina was maybe seven weeks old; she had been on the monitor and the doctor had also changed her formula to lactose free. My sister was saying that the sleep apnea machine was making sores on her belly and that Sebrina was fine now and the machine needed to go back. They told my sister they would be coming to pick it up. They came alright, with DFS and the cops, and took Sebrina to a foster home. I will never forget it. I was frying chicken. After they took my niece, no one could eat. My sister got clean, got a job and an apartment and took every parenting class she could to get her back. She got her back when she was ten months old.

It was around that time Mark moved back to Buffalo. Him and Momma broke up and Momma was happy working at the local girl's shelter taking care of under-age girls who didn't have permanent placement. She really loved it and she was good at it.

My sister Roci and my nephew Alex moved to Wellsville, KS, to get away from the meth epidemic in Springfield. It is still a huge problem all across the US. Charlie, Dylan and Sebrina's dad around this time got caught with a mobile meth lab and ended up in a very long standoff with police. He had fallen asleep in the attic. It made front page news. He ended up do-ing thirteen years in the Federal prison system. Roci just wanted a better life for her and Alex, and I don't blame her for that. It hurt a lot because I was nana to all my nephews and baby niece Sebrina. What a joy to me when she came home.

Sebrina came home and my sister had her apart-ment and job, but almost immediately met Steve at the bar down the street from her house. I would stay with Dylan and Sebrina. I would sing "Amazing Grace" to Sebrina. I loved putting bows on her bald cute head, with her big rosy cheeks, and her big dimples. She was everything to me. My sister would stay at Steve's house most nights and I would just keep the house clean and watch Sebrina. Dylan was in Head Start. I got to stay at her apartment and have just my close friends over. I did calm down. I was smart enough to know it wouldn't take much for DFS to come knocking. Soon my sister found out she was pregnant with what would be my youngest nephew, Zachary. My sister moved in with Steve and gave up her apartment. Zachary was born November 16, 1998, I was seventeen.

I had been working for Savage Tech (they sold vacuums) where I was hired on the spot when I was sixteen as the phone room manager, setting appointments for demonstrations of the vacuum. We would give them a three-day, two-night stay in Branson, MO or somewhere else—you know the next timeshare scheme—on top of a $3000.00 vacuum. Well, the company was awesome, the product was great, we worked hard, and we played harder. Every month we would go to KC for a big pep talk meeting at the Doubletree conference center. I was surrounded by professionals, not thugs, and for once I felt inspired! I loved sales! I loved motivating my phone room and giving them hourly breaks. I gave everyone a chance, and $9.00 an hour in 1997 / 1998 was good money.

My momma was making $7.00 an hour so I helped her with bills and had a satellite dish installed in her house. Momma loved to time record movies. It was an everyday thing, that a sticky note would be on our console TV saying "Do not touch VCR! SET TO RECORD!" Momma loved to collect things. Our home was full of bookshelves with lots of books in paperback and a lot of the same ones in hardback. Momma had her favorites. My favorite times with Momma watching movies was when she had read the book and they made it into a movie. Momma would say in the beginning, "Oh, this is going to be good if it's anything like the book." I couldn't wait till the credits ended to hear Momma's version. It was even more fun when I was older and we would smoke pot and get munchies and watch movies and just hang out. She collected books, movies (she kept an alphabetized notebook of them), owls, tea sets, and at one point TV guides, but she stopped collecting those and told us later she didn't care for owls. We just kept getting them for her and so did everyone else so she didn't want to hurt anyone's feelings. She later in her late fifties decided elephants was her thing and it soon became mine too. I LOVE ELEPHANTS. I had bought my momma several elephant figurines and she picked this one for me to get tattooed on me for her. Our favorite color is the same: RED. I just love red. We both want red everything!

I was seventeen living in a townhouse with a girl I hired at the vacuum job and things were going well. I was selling pot to get even more money and my home-boys Orlando and Eric came over and I was showing them my new spot. I was living nice and had matching furniture that was paid for. We were drinking and playing spades and listening to music. I could tell Eric was acting funny. I realized later I had gotten robbed for all my money I had hidden upstairs where my only bathroom was. I knew they were both on meth because they had both been on that shit since making that first trip to Colorado. But I knew for a fact it was Eric. I found out years later because he would do this to me again, except the next time I was going to be ready.

I hurried up and got back right with my money and was still keeping in contact with Bobby. I met these guys from St. Louis at the gas station. We will call them Tree and his friend Larry. It didn't take me two minutes to realize they were some dope boys down there getting money. They were fine and so were me and all my home girls. I thought *Hmm... let's see what happens here.* I started talking to Tree but more on a money tip because he would pay me to hold all their 'work', the whole crew's crack! Like a lot! It never occurred to me I could get caught, and I didn't. I never sold it or wanted to. My thing was pot. After all, daddy said that was death, and I felt like I didn't have any business learning that trade. I was working, selling weed, and getting paid to hold their drugs. I didn't need nothing else. I had a nice clean ass blue 88 Lincoln town car when I turned eighteen, that I bought myself. It was actually my third car I had bought myself. It was just the nicest.

At this point I had switched back to living at my mommas. It was cheaper and I could help her with bills. I was still at the vacuum company, and it was the annual picnic in Denver. We as a company would drive up together and go to the huge water park for the big picnic. Then management was invited to the CEO's million-dollar home for an elite party that happened to be next door to an NFL player's house. It was like nothing I had seen in my eighteen years. I had long ago decided I would work my ass off really hard to be rich and famous. I was game for vacuums or whatever God had planned for me. I believed in God my whole life. I was just angry with him ever since that day in court. I thought God had too many people to hear me, so I thought I was on my own and I just stopped talking to him. BOY OH BOY WAS I VERY WRONG!

My sister was now a single mom of three: Dylan, Sebrina, and Zachary. They were my world. I spoiled them and kept them often, especially Sebrina. At some point my best friend Amanda V started dating Big B. He was Tree's big brother and they moved their stuff to their place. Thank God I dodged that Federal offense. Geez, to look back as I write this, I must say Dear God I was such an idiot and it's going to get worse, oh so much worse before it gets better.

I started working at a water softener company and was the assistant phone room manager. We would call to set appointments for people to get their water tested and we would give you a coupon book. I am actually very passionate about water. I learned a lot about high quality H_2O, like why ice cubes at home have frozen white looking powder that is frozen dirt and unknown particles, I will stick with clear ice cubes. I worked for them on and off the next four years. I was now eighteen and I could visit Bobby in prison. He sent me legal mail (no one is supposed to be able to read it). Honestly, I wasn't even thinking of the consequences at all, I really never did think of them. This was a trend. Bobby wasn't just wanting me to visit him. He wanted me to bring pot in orange balloons, as many as I could fit in my vagina, dime size. He said once I got past security, I should go to the ladies room and pull them out to put them in my pocket. All visitors had to purchase the snacks. He told me to get any orange chips and when he came to visit, after we got our hug, at the beginning of the visitation to hand him the chips. He would open them, and I would very discreetly get the pot filled balloons out of my pocket and act as if I was reaching for a chip and drop them in, and he would eat them. I absolutely felt a connection to my dad because I found out that when my dad was in prison my grandpa and my dad's friend used to go visit him and when they were able to bring him homemade food his friend would sneak pot into him through the food. My grandfather had no clue he was smuggling in pot to my dad.

Me and Bobby were making plans to be together when he got released. Now we are all caught up. I'm 19. I had just broken up with Antonio for cheating on me and kicked him out in twenty-one inches of snow and I had slept with Bobby. I was extremely heartbroken over Tonio. I was heartbroken and had mixed feelings about loving and hating my dad. I had a really good friend Marlon come over he was my pot plug and just a good friend. He brought blunts and a bottle of E&J liquor and we just drank and hung out as buddies. I was kind of like my momma, had lots of friends, men and women. My friend Orlando was one, and still is one that I can call anytime day or night. He will just listen to me cry and he will rescue me if I need it. If he can help or his girlfriend can, they will. I cherish that friendship. I was still working through all of that, and the breakup happened the morning of December 7, 2000.

I was at work first week or so of January and was feeling sick and started wondering if I could be pregnant. I took a test at a friend's house. Yes, I was in fact pregnant! The word of the day was FUCK! I counted back and yep, I got pregnant the week of the December 7. It was too close to say exactly who the dad was. I didn't really give a shit. At that point all I needed to know was that the baby was mine. I didn't want to be with either one of those lying cheaters!

I stopped working through my pregnancy because I was so sick all the time. I couldn't eat anything at all. It was the worst. One day I wanted boiled eggs (but only the yellow part). I wanted sweet coco. I got so sick! NEVER again in my life! I couldn't even eat biscuits and gravy, and that's my favorite. I lost twenty-one lbs. my first trimester. I told my OBGYN that smoking pot seemed to help a little and he said it was fine and that I needed to gain weight.

Antonio and Bobby both wanted to be with me and both really thought or hoped my baby was theirs. I felt more comfortable with Tonio and was in love with him. We had known each other since age thirteen and had been friends for such a long time, and we had already built a life together. I was thinking of Bobby and what he did, putting me at risk to bring him pot into the prison and his constant lifestyle. I didn't want my child to have that kind of life if I could give it better. Antonio hustled, but he also worked a real job. All Bobby did was sell crack and that zebra never changed his stripes. Me and Antonio started working things out. Before I knew it, it was March 11, and I turned 20.

Me and my stepmom Kitty had a huge falling out just a few weeks after my dad died. At that time, I was still thinking it was a hunting accident. It wouldn't be until the year I turned twenty-seven that I found out different by speaking with a Missouri conservation agent that was first on the scene. He said there is no way possible it was an accident, and it was still an open case. However, it would never legally be solved. But I know exactly what I suspect happened. The agent told me my dad was hunting with my stepbrother Jeff, who is now deceased, but it was my dad, a friend of his, and my stepbrother who was fifteen years old older than me. Jeff hated my dad, probably for good reason, but still. A justified defense I could understand, but they planned this. It made sense finally. The agent told me my dad was shooting a 30/30 mag and Jeff had a twenty-two and remember what my dad's friends' gun was because what he would say next was shocking. He said my dad had just shot a deer and put a hole in the deer the size of a coffee can, and I had been told by my stepmom that Dad was lowering his gun from the tree stand (which is normal) and it slipped, hit the ground, went off, and the bullet lodged in his left shoulder, kind of close to his heart. I had gone out to my dad's a couple weeks after he died just to visit, and Kitty made it really clear I wasn't welcome there. She made me leave and at the time I did not have my car (it was broken down), but she wanted me gone. I will never forget leaving my family's ma and pop old closed down family store and home, that was in my dad's family for generations, and walking, crying my eyes out down 64 HWY with a brand-new pack of cigarettes and no fucking lighter! I had walked to the next small country store and called Inez collect, bawling my eyes out. I believe she did 80 mph to get to me. When she got there, she just held me!

I found out my stepmom got over $250,000.00 and all the land (which the bitch sold). The new owners turned it into a junkyard! I can still close my eyes and see my grandpa picking walnuts and see my great-grandma Larkin pruning her roses. My stepmom had plenty of motive to have her son shoot my dad while they were hunting. The agent told me he took my dad's gun to the station and banged it against the concrete several times and could never get it to go off. My dad was only thirty-nine with no will. I was nineteen so I couldn't get anything without a will. My dad told me over a million times I'm sure, 'I DONT GOT MUCH, BUT WHAT I DO GOT IS YOURS WHEN I DIE.' Honestly, I didn't care about the money. My family's land is what I did care about. I respected my stepmom and her position as his wife and wouldn't have put her out ever. I would have always understood if my dad was killed in self-defense—I prepared myself for that years ago—but to murder him and bury Jeff in her plot next to him was just morbid. It really bothered me. But years and years of severe abuse will really fuck anyone up.

CHAPTER EIGHT

I was about four months pregnant, and I found out Antonio was doing meth occasionally behind my back, because he knew I thought it was not ok to do and the only thing it was good for was to make money. We ain't junkies, we don't smoke up money! That's a big no-no in the hustle world. This became a huge problem in our relationship. He would stay gone for a couple days at a time. One time I got in the car and started driving around looking for him. I had gotten a call from my friend CeCe that was dating his friend and she told me he was coming out of the bathroom with a girl. I flipped out and proceeded to drive everywhere. I couldn't find him at any of his usual hangouts, and then—boom! — we were passing each other, going opposite directions on the same street

He pulled into a fast-food place. He had his best friend Cox's girlfriend Shelly with him in a S10 truck I had never seen before. I got out the car yelling, asking him what the fuck was going on and he immediately backed up to drive off! I was furious. He went around the drive thru and I jumped my pregnant ass in the back of that truck and reached in from behind and started punching him, telling him to pull this bitch over NOW!!! So he did and I jumped out the truck and we were yelling back and forth and he started laughing at me and making fun of me while chugging a can of beer at 8am. I punched him, and a cop came out of what seemed nowhere and grabbed me, and he drove off. It was a female cop. I told her what was going on and she let me go with a warning. I can't believe how angry I would get sometimes and while pregnant. Shame on me. Thank God my baby was ok and very healthy.

My pregnancy was constant stress due to Tonio smoking meth and leaving, and we found out I was having a girl. I was hoping for a boy, but Kayden was on her way into this world. I had nephews and nieces I adored, but NOTHING could prepare me for motherhood. I was terrified of raising a daughter. When I found out it was a girl, my brain immediately went to someday somebody's going to hurt her and I'm going to have to kill them because the police don't help, the court system for sure don't, and it just is what it is. I even told Antonio while lying in bed one night while I was pregnant that if I even had a thought that he touched my baby wrong I would kill him first and ask questions later. Antonio replied with, "I understand," which made me love him more. It also in some way made me feel safe. I needed him to understand my fear was real. He did understand. For the most part me and

Antonio had a very loving magical relationship and agreed on everything, except his drug use that often led to cheating and of course fighting.

I was almost seven months pregnant, and my momma had extra movie tickets for free movie passes, so me and Tonio went on a date. We went to see *What's the Worst That Could Happen*. Well, it did! Tonio got drunk before we went to the movies with his best friend Boston and my oldest sister and they were being so belligerent. Tonio had smuggled in a few beer bottles and was constantly yelling and being obnoxious, so I moved up closer to the front away from all of them. I was big and pregnant and wearing a new dress and new cute sandals. It was summertime and I was due at the beginning of September. I was sitting there trying to ignore them and all of a sudden, I hear them all laughing because Tonio was telling Boston he peed in his empty beer bottle and he was encouraging him to do the same instead of going to the bathroom. Well, you know how a theater slopes down as you get closer to the screen? The next thing I knew, I heard the sound of a beer bottle rolling down the concrete theater floor, then my sandals and even my feet had Tonio's urine all over them! I was so fucking pissed! I got up and walked the fuck out, got in my car. Tonio followed me and got in the car with me. I told him I was going the fuck home to take a shower right now! He said to take him to his friend Austin's. I said, "I'm not taking you no fucking where except home you can figure it out from there!" I was driving at this time almost 40 mph and he out of no-where just elbows the fuck out of me in my jaw. Thank God we did not wreck. I got the car stopped and pulled over. I made him get out! I was holding a giant soda, and it was everywhere: all over the ceiling of my car, on me, all in my hair, my face, my clothes. I had pee on my feet and new sandals, and my jaw hurt so fucking bad! It actually still pops to this day from that elbow. I called Bobby and told him what happened, and he brought me a thirty-eight revolver. He was doing the same old shit just a new day and more money and was moving around to different states but making fast moves.

My friend CeCe came and saw me. She had dated Tonio's brother, and I knew the dynamic of the abuse she went through with him that their mother would watch and never say anything about. Many times, it was near death experiences. I saw some myself. What's funny is he, Tonio's brother, had a daughter with my best friend Twila and was never anything but sweet to her. Well CeCe came because she not only heard Tonio had put his hands on me while I was pregnant, and we broke up, but CeCe came to tell me that Tonio had gotten a girl preg-nant. I knew her well; it was the girl we all used for rides and the one Tonio used to steal clothes from. When I say I couldn't wear windbreaker pants because it made him think about her annoying ass it is true. She acted like she was my friend, and I would catch her in lies all the time.

I gave birth to Kayden at 12:15am on August 28, 2001. She weighed 6lbs1oz. She was absolutely beautiful, I know all moms say that, but my babies were all extremely beautiful. Mixed babies usually are. All of our friends were at the hospital for a pre-birth party. Literally coolers full of beer on ice in the parking lot and most of my friends had two or more babies. To be twenty and a new momma was late in my generation. Amanda was the last of us to actually get pregnant, but Kayden was perfect! I remember visiting hours were over and everyone was asked to leave, and they got me back to my room with Kayden. My friend CeCe snuck up there and made it in to visit Kayden and me. I loved CeCe a lot. It's sad what ended up happening to her in life.

We brought Kayden home and Bobby came over. He called me from his car phone and said he wanted to see Kayden, that he heard she looked like him. I told him she didn't. To me she did look like Tonio. Tonio did not want to know and said he believed she was his. So Bobby came in and said, "Nope she don't look like me," and spoke to my momma and left.

Things were going really well with our little family. We stayed home and hung out playing dominoes, spades games and dice, when everyone was home from work. My job at that time was just to take care of Kayden and hustle a little pot while Tonio worked and hustled harder stuff, but just a little on the side, and Momma was still working at the shelter. We were living good. Momma worked twelve hours over night, so it felt like we lived alone every other week, and we had space from each other. We got along great. Tonio and

Momma really bonded. Tonio's mom was a crackhead who never was a real mother. No holidays or birthdays or anything of the sort was celebrated. Unless his granny did for him, he didn't get anything. My momma treated him like a son, and I will never forget our Christmases together.

Momma would end up taking Tonio Christmas shopping and he would pick stuff out for me to surprise me with. They did a great job. He got me a hope chest, I still have it. He also got me comfy pajamas and my favorite candy and perfume that was very expensive. I had never received such amazing gifts. Momma never had money to spend on the things she would have wanted to get us. She would wrap anything to make a gift under the tree. I got a can of black olives every year and me and my sisters and the whole family got those intense super sweet chocolate covered cherries. I would infuse them with vodka, or rum! Ha, but I'm in recovery now. You normies try that. Anyway, holidays became Antonio's favorite times, not something to dread.

Eventually, we decided to move out and get apartments in the same complex. Instead of staying in the old two-bedroom house we would get Momma in a one-bedroom apartment and us a two-bedroom. My friend Laura lived underneath us in our building. Momma lived in the building next to ours. Tonio's mom needed a place to stay, and Laura was pregnant with her third child and could use a roommate, so she let her rent a room.

It was the beginning of March 2002 and the week right before my twenty-first birthday. My birthday twin that I met at the water softener company was having wine with me at our apartment while Kayden, who was six months old, was sleeping in her crib. Tonio was downstairs visiting his mom. I didn't think anything about it. It was normal for him to visit his mom, right? Well Laura came upstairs and told me, "Um Hannah, Tonio and his mom are smoking crack in her room in my apartment. Laura said Tonios' mom had gotten a call and when she knocked on his mom's bedroom door to hand her the phone, she said it smelled like they were smoking crack. Laura immediately came upstairs to tell me and she was obviously very angry and I was also very furious, I was embarrassed and ashamed! I honestly thought we were past this bullshit. I told Laura, "Don't even tell him I know anything."

Laura went back down to her apartment and my friend left. Soon Tonio came home, upstairs. I asked him if he wanted to have sex (coke/crack makes most guys impotent). He replied, "Nah not right now." I said, "Yea, I want to give you head!" He said, "No I'm not in the mood." I said, "Why you been sucking glass dick with your mom!? Are you a fucking crackhead like her?" He began to beat me like I was trying to kill him or something. He grabbed a mirror off the wall, busted it over my whole face and threw me on the ground and stomped on me so many times over and over again for what seemed like forever! He ripped the phone cords out the wall so I couldn't call for help. When he was finally done, I was lying in the fetal position on the floor bald up bleeding and crying from the severity of the beating he just gave me. He came into the bedroom and told me to clean myself up and come into the living room. He was rolling a blunt. He wanted me to smoke it with him. I did what he asked best I could because my face and throat was bleeding. He finally left. I ran to Laura's apartment, because my momma was working the overnight shift. I banged on Laura's door and Tonio's mom answered the door to. She saw me bloody and beaten to shit. She said, "I'm so sick of y'all fighting on Friday nights." I pray Tonio's mother gets exactly what she deserves and I have no desire to ever have her in my or my kids lives ever. God is good and he will deal with her. She will never be a part of my life.

I finally got Laura woke up and got the phone and called my momma. My momma took emergency leave from work. I refused to call the police—what were they going to do? The police had never helped me before and I was not taking the chance of getting DFS involved because Kayden was there when it happened, and we fought over him smoking crack. That's a big no! I don't trust the police! After Laura got me cleaned up it was just a lot of little cuts on my throat and face and bruising, I was just really sore. My momma got there and called my sister Roci. By that time, she had been married and was going through a divorce. But Roci came immediately that night and got me and Kayden and all our stuff and moved us to Willsville, KS. Life changed quickly, in less than twelve hours. Life is funny like that, or scary.

CHAPTER NINE

Wellsville, KS, was a very small town with literally two gas stations, and they really had brick roads. It made Buffalo look like a giant city. Me and Kayden were safe at Roci and Alex's house. I was so happy to be around my oldest nephew. He was a big kid now. He was nana's boy more than ever and loved his cousin, baby Kayden. The first few days were so hard. I was in so much pain. I couldn't even hold Kayden. I had Tonio's footprint bruised into my chest. My twenty-first birthday, March 11, came and we kind of celebrated at Roci's, but I was in so much pain. Eventually I physically felt better and got a job at one of the convenience/gas stations in town. It was also the main hangouts for old folks to sip their morning coffee and shoot the shit. It was my job to open up at 3am and start making donuts, breakfast sandwiches, and to start lunch stuff around 9am before my shift ended at 10am. It was a unique job that I would not desire to do again. It was creepy being there so early by myself pulling stuff from the cooler—almost too quiet.

It was probably June when I started missing my friends. I had been missing my momma. Momma said she wanted me and Kayden to come and move in with her in her apartment so we did. Tonio, my new EVIL MONSTER HERO, was still living in our old apartment. We talked a few times while I was up there. He sent me a few dollars, I think once, and said how sorry he was, but was acting like he wanted to do drugs and that's just how it was going to be. He actually said if I could not accept it, we couldn't be together. So I said, "Okay, WE ARE NOT GOING TO BE TOGETHER!"

I was living at Momma's apartment. I was there for a week and Tonio called me and asked me if he could make my twenty-first birthday up to me and take me out, just us. I thought about it and didn't see any harm in eating a nice meal and spending his money. So I decided to go on the date. We went to eat, and to a pool hall, and had drinks—a lot of drinks. I remember getting picked up by Cox and Boston's baby Momma. It's safe to say I was completely drunk. I remember being in the car maybe a mile at most from home, and next thing I knew Cox was picking me up off the pavement at our apartment complex. Tonio had drug me out the car, stomped all over my face and chest. I was all bloody. To this day don't remember what happened to make him snap. No one did. Cox carried me into my momma's apartment. He carried me to the bathroom. There was a tiny pebble rock embedded in my nose. He cleaned me up, but he had warrants, and with all the commotion the cops surely were on the way. Cox carried me to the couch and laid me there, on his way out he left my door wide open, and I was laying there crying in so much pain.

Soon an officer approached my door and peeked in. My light was on bright. Viewing me laying there crying on the couch, all he said was, "Where is the white guy, bald head, red basketball shorts?" I said, "I just got beat up by my baby daddy, but that's not him." The officer just walked away and acted like I didn't exist. This was another time the system failed me and my family! The next day I went to the ER. I had a broken nose and two big black eyes, bruised ribs and my front tooth was chipped, and his footprints were once again bruised into my chest. I called Tonio after I left the hospital because I needed money for medicine and told him to have Boston get me the money because I didn't want to see Tonio at that time. But Tonio came anyway and started bawling crying at the sight of me, just crying uncontrollably. But for me it was over, and I meant it this time. He even said he would quit drugs and I said, "NOPE!"

I went back to work from 5pm to 9pm making full time money selling long distance services. The money was great. I really loved long distance telephone sales. I was pretty good at it. As long as I would buy the products, I would sell it! I made Top Seller for both full and part-time shifts on sales per hour for the quarter most quarters. They used my calls in their training classes for our large recruit classes they had weekly. So I was doing good. Me, Kayden, and Momma had a townhouse at a really fun townhome village and apartment complex, with two huge pools. One pool was shaped like Mickey Mouse. It had kid's playgrounds and tennis courts, and BBQ pits. It was really a wonderful place! We were very happy, and I had even started dating and going to the clubs in my free time. Tonio ended up doing ninety days in jail at some point. We weren't on speaking terms even though Barbara would have a son with him and was now dating Boston and felt the need to constantly contact me.

I was busy making money and having fun with Kayden and my niece and nephews. I kept Dylan, Sebrina and Zachary a lot. Roci would let Alex spend summers and we would spend them at the mouse shaped pool. Having BBQs and lots of fun and always music and card games were what you would find us doing. Tori from Buffalo even lived down a few apartment complexes and she would bring her son and a lot of us, Twila, and my nieces would come and we just had a blast!

Tonio got out and started five years' probation soon after and did not want to go to prison. He also wanted to be with me. We had technically been split up since March of 2002. It was October 2002, so seven months, and I was not interested in being with him at all. I was happy with my single life. He would come over every day doing nice shit just to irritate me. He knew I hated taking out the trash and that I thought it was a man's job, so he would show up just for that and of course to see Kayden. He always wanted to take me shopping, not just give me money. He always wanted to take me to eat and try to rent me a movie I liked, like a rom com, he normally wouldn't agree to just to hopefully score happy points. But I got him when we got to my place. I told him I didn't want to watch the movie and he needed to leave. I kept telling him I didn't want to be with him and I was glad he was off crack and meth and only drank now, but I couldn't do it. He got really upset when I hired my cousin to fix my alternator because I did not want to see my ex every day! It was bad enough we had a kid. He would even come over every day to take out my trash. It was too much. He would not help me if I did not spend time with him, so I put him on child support. After I told him that he backed off.

I went about my life for the next couple of months. It was maybe mid-January 2003 and me and Tonio started being more friendly on his visits with Kayden and actually getting along. He had been clean since July when he went to jail, so he had six good months. He was on probation. This could work now. We start dating again. He got me a huge diamond ring with nineteen diamonds in it. He bought it from a crack-head. It was so nice! We had just gotten back together. We got the DNA results: "Antonio Draper IS NOT THE FATHER!" HE WAS SO CRUSHED, but we knew the chances. Barbara's son was his. I believed I said it could go this way, well it did. I contacted Bobby and let him know. He hung up on me. I went and found him at a club and took Kayden's pictures to him. He denied her. I petitioned for his DNA. The test came back: he was NOT THE FATHER!!!!!!!!!

What the actual fuck? Now I was very confused! It was probably two weeks or so later, one of my best girlfriends, Gerdy, who was actually living in the same townhouses as me, calls me telling me that a friend we know, Cheryl, is dating Bobby's cousin and Bobby and his cousin got into a huge fight about his cousin smoking up all the 'work crack.' His cousin screamed out, 'What about that paternity test I took for you?' Cheryl immediately called Gerdy. Within five minutes of Gerdy calling and informing me of this information we were on our way to the child support office. I told them what I had heard, they showed me the picture of the man they took the DNA from, and it was not Bobby! I was beyond angry! The lady told me she couldn't give me any information on him and then she slid his folder that was open toward me. I memorized the address on file. I left and went straight there. I didn't know exactly which apartment, but I did find his silver tricked out SUV sitting on 24s. I wrote him a note and left it on the window saying, "You raggedy lying bitch how dare you have your cousin take the DNA test? You best get a hold of me ASAP!" He called about an hour and a half later. He said, "When are you bringing my daughter to come see me?" Seriously, I was thinking *Is this motherfucker psychotic?* I told him I did need to speak with Antonio because he has been a daddy this whole time and that Tonio already respected my decision to have them both be there for Kayden. It's ok she has two dads that love her, so give me a day and we will come for a visit the next day.

I wasn't prepared the next day for Bobby to tell me the reason he did the DNA test like that was because he had already caught a career criminal Federal crack cocaine case and was waiting on the feds to pick him up. I wasn't shocked. But I would definitely be shocked when my home boy Marlon, who was my pot plug and home boy forever, came over to the townhouse and threw the black and white paperwork down from when the feds just kicked his momma's house in and at the top, under "Confidential informant," was Bobby's full name. I had no idea they even knew each other. I found out later, when Marlon told me he and Bobby both had family or people in common from Beam Street Bloods out of St. Louis, MO.

It was February 2003 and me and Tonio were ok. He told me he wanted a baby and I think I literally got pregnant the night he said it. I was not ready to have another baby. I was scared. My last pregnancy was not the greatest experience. I almost did not have the baby, but Tonio begged me to have his baby and I couldn't go through with the abortion after I heard the heart-beat. Tonio's drinking was annoying and obnoxious but no physical violence at all. But that Halloween, I was nine months pregnant, with Kayden twenty-six months old, trick or treating with Twila and her kids, and I got back to the townhouse and Tonio was gone. It was a Friday evening. Where could he be? I looked for him everywhere by phone, and nothing all weekend. I then realized he was probably at Austin and Catherine's house in Branson with some bitch, and I drove up there. I got up there and he was there all right.

He wouldn't let me out the car. He kept calling me a stupid bitch, laughing at me and telling me to leave. He was leaning on my car door. I told him I was going to go drive off a fucking bridge, fuck this whole fucking world! I have no idea, except God himself above, looking back, how I got home on that forty-five-minute drive from Branson back to Springfield. I did make it back home and I got in my bed and screamed and cried like I was four years old. I remember screaming to my dad, "YOU MEAN PIECE OF SHIT, THIS IS WHEN I NEED YOU TO HELP ME WITH LIFE. TO PROTECT FROM MEN LIKE YOU. I DIDN'T NEED YOU WHEN I WAS LITTLE. I FUCKING NEED YOU NOW DAD!" Soon I stopped crying and calmed down a lot and was just lying there. It was maybe fifteen minutes later I heard Tonio come up the stairs and crawl in bed and I just stayed silent. I didn't speak to him at all. We just went to sleep.

The next morning, we woke up and he comes and starts telling me to tell my dad to leave him alone. I was like, "What? Wait! What?" He looked at me like I was crazy. I said, "What do you mean? What exactly happened?" He said, "I feel what I think is your dad breathing down my neck all the time, especially when I do my work clothes every day and walk downstairs." He also said, "And last night I had a dream he was staring at me with two big ass pit bulls, one on each side of him." I had never told Tonio my dad used to breed pit bulls. I couldn't help but actually feel happy and safe and I felt my dad was with me, just because I couldn't see him and it had been a long time since I smelled his smell (something like skoal, oil and gunpowder and animal blood). Yep, those were the smells I think of when I think of dad, unless we were going to a steakhouse, then it was skoal, Irish spring, and gunpowder. So I explained to Tonio what happened when I got back and I told him good and to watch his back because Dad was not to be fucked with! "Better treat his daughter how you want ours treated."

Kaleah, 7lbs 14oz, would be born November 22, 2003, at 11:23am, by C-section. It definitely was not our birth plan. The C-section seemed like forever. I just wanted to hear her cry. It seemed so weird. I could feel the pressure of them moving my guts around. It didn't hurt but was extremely awkward. Finally, I heard her cry, but because they had this weird tarp up to protect me, I guess from me seeing my guts laid out, now I wanted to see her. Tonio saw her. She was so pale with bright red hair and big red ruby lips she was and still is the perfect mixture of me and Antonio. Healing up from a C-section is also a lot harder on your body.

One thing I will always say is Tonio definitely was a great dad to all the kids. Also, a great uncle and brother-in-law. He had no problem always taking care of the girls, just as much as me. We were basically already living like we were a married couple, and we battled a lot of shit. My oldest sister married a guy younger than her, straight out of prison, that she didn't even know. His name was Terry, and he was some skinhead racist that I believe was actually my age. It was her life, but he took her for a spin, immediately had her sell everything she owned to move to Colorado. That lasted a month or so, they came back, and she was pregnant. They moved in our basement, then moved out after scamming Momma into writing some hot checks. Then Momma went a little crazy and it kicked off right before the holidays. My momma lost her mind when she saw her checks would pass anywhere. I have no idea how much we actually spent together, but I helped Momma pay all the ones back that hit the bad check department and I personally gave her over $8,000.00, because yes, I was right there spending the checks on Momma's account with her. It was fun at the time because Momma had never ever had money to buy just anything she wanted, but it was gluttony and uncalled for is how I feel now. Today I feel differently and would not condone 90% of my actions, but that 10% is a motherfucker I tell ya!

My sister and her husband moved out with Dylan, Sebrina, and Zachary and Heather was pregnant with my niece Harley that was due to come mid-May. I was very worried because Terry was very mean to the boys. I could not handle the way he talked to my little nephews, and I spoke up like, "Excuse me you don't tell a three-year-old not to punk you out! Because he is going to eat his dinner" (Zachary was always a very picky eater). He would stand over poor little Zachary with his fists clenched in a punching position. He would tell Zachary that he had him fucked up. These were my babies. I been helping my sister their whole life and I always will and to this day I'm still there for them.

My sister and her husband and the kids moved out. It was the beginning of summer 2004. Me and Tonio were both twenty-three and our relationship had never been better. We were both working and hadn't had a breakup or a bad fight since that Halloween, and I felt safe and secure, and I would for a while. My sister was almost due with Harley, and they were homeless again. She didn't want to stay with us, they just wanted us to take Dylan, Sebrina, and Zachary. Me, Antonio, and Momma said of course. Alex would be coming when school let out in KC where him and Roci were now living. We had a house full. Twila was in and out of prison so I would relieve Inez of babysitting a lot or when I could because between Tonio's kids, our kids and our niece and three nephews, we had nine kids most days from three months to age nine. We were overwhelmed with kiddos. We loved it. The more the merrier.

We moved into a bigger house before the summer ended, with a huge back deck and it was covered and amazing. We all loved it. I dug a BBQ pit in the backyard and put rocks in it and a giant metal fridge, grates on top. It was the best grill I ever cooked on. Everyone came running when they got the word we were having a BBQ. Not going to lie, I do throw down. My momma taught me, or rather just passed down the ability to simply be able to know how to cook. I fried chicken breast on the bone, made mashed potatoes, gravy, and corn biscuits for the first time when I was 10 years old by myself, because my momma had gone on a float trip, and I knew she would be hungry when she got home. I started cooking Christmas dinner when I was seventeen by myself, because Roci moved away and Heather just wouldn't.

My sister Heather would go through extreme changes. She battled mental illness and addiction and it all played a part in making her seem like a monster to me and my family. I continued to pray for my sister and hoped one day she would be back to my sister I grew up with that had always been my hero. I was missing that Heather so much!

CHAPTER TEN

It was Christmas Eve 2004. I had to get up early and go get my check, do my last bit of shopping, pick up bikes for Kayden and Kaleah, and get stocking stuffers. I was so excited, I jump up, kissed Tonio, jumped in the freezing car and got halfway around the block. I was lighting my first cigarette of the morning and oh my, I had to stop the car, I was so sick for like five minutes. I grabbed a pregnancy test, a cheap one, for $1.00. I've got two kids in this world already and had a miscarriage a few months back. But come on seriously, it's Christmas Eve! So I finished up all my shopping and went home. I was so curious; it was driving me crazy. So I took the test. Tonio was lying on the couch with Kaleah and she was napping. He was just watching TV and I just handed him a positive pregnancy test and said, "Merry CHRISTMAS!!" I walked away and let that shock set in as it did for me and went and wrapped presents.

Now we had outgrown a three-bedroom house. The landlord didn't want to fix anything, I couldn't even do laundry at our house because he wouldn't fix whatever was wrong with the power and water in the laundry room. Also, we had another baby coming and would eventually need more room, so started looking for a larger place. If we had a boy like we were really hoping for, either way we needed a separate nursery for the baby because Kaleah and Kayden who was starting Head Start were going to be turning two and four years old. We got a little over $9000.00 in taxes back and had found a house with two living rooms, three bedrooms, and a screened-in sunroom with a fenced in backyard. It was perfect. It had a double electric garage and was perfect for a pool in the back and my BBQ parties. We got it and had plenty of time to move in slowly. We had keys, and everything was set.

In the house as usual packing up for the move a little bit, I had grabbed a quarter pound of pot from the new connection since Marlon got five years in the fed when Bobby turned state's evidence. My best friend Twila brought my nieces Kensley and Hailey up. They were going to stay at my place and we were going to take all the kids to the pizza buffet arcade and have some fun. I knew Twila had not checked in with her parole officer, so I was trying to spend time with her before she got locked back up because Twila ended up doing about seven years somehow on a five-year sentence because she kept absconding. So Twila's youngest baby's father was with her and all the kids were asleep, so we took a ride over to the new house and her boyfriend stayed there and watched the kids while we took a simple load of the kids' yard toys. Also, I wanted to go with my best friend, smoke a blunt over there and christen the new spot because we never got time alone with just us.

It was a beautiful home. It had skylights in the living room. We weren't at the new house long and literally felt surrounded in a creepy way. I had NEVER felt this way. Something had to be wrong with this house, like haunted, maybe? All I knew was, we had to get out of that house quickly! Me and Twila got in the car that I had pulled into our new attached garage and I was shaking. I was so freaked out and scared. I was thinking how are we going to live in a haunted house? But that feeling stayed with me as I was driving us back to my house. I started the car before opening the garage and I heard that was very dangerous but not near as dangerous as this feeling I had. Twila was acting normal. She was fiddling with the music, but the feeling stayed with me. I was driving to our current house and I turned down the Main Street that my street was off of. About ten to fifteen vehicles of all kinds—station wagons, escorts, big cars, little cars, trucks, you name it—followed me, they were all behind me. It was no Taurus like I heard cops use as unmarked cars. I thought maybe there was a function at the school, but not after 10pm. I came to an intersection and a cop was ahead of me, but he turned off. I proceeded forward to my street. The cars started dispersing in different directions. I started to feel better.

I turned on my street and everything was normal, mind you the whole time Twila was completely ok and at ease, cool as a fucking cucumber! We get out the car. I say out loud, "Girl this weed must be fire to have me tripping like that." I had a split second to notice my doorknob was gone, and BOOM! What seemed like the Taliban, jumped off my roof, came out my front door, came running out of bushes. It was extremely intense! Twila yelled out, "Are you here for me?" This was something out of the movies. To be honest yes, we sold pot, always did, mostly to people who was my family, or I considered my family. It helped me smoke for free and make a few bucks. Me, my momma and Tonio all had jobs outside the home. I was actually back at the water softener company.

"Crack and guns!" That's what they kept screaming!!! "Where's the crack? Where are the guns, DAMMIT!!! We know Antonio keeps it in your house!" I was so confused, especially how they had taken me in my room and were screaming at me, telling me they knew I was lying because they had found bullets in my room, and we were in my room. They talked like Tonio didn't live with me and he had for two years and had worked the same job that whole time with my address. We didn't get assistance; we were clearly living together. They spent what looked like thousands for me to tell them, while they were beating the shit out of Twila and her boyfriend for her lying and using her kid's name. But they had all our kids awake lined up, even my little nephew Zachary was spending the night. The kids lined up on the couch just listening to Twila getting beat and screaming from the police and her boyfriend too for lying for her. I would soon realize the room they were referring to was actually my momma's room, where they had actually found an old buck shot of my dad's (he used to reload them, had a whole setup). My momma kept them as a memento of the hero part of my dad, the part she loved when everything was ok for those brief times.

Well, we had no crack and no guns! They were many years too late to catch crack in my house, so I told them straight up, "I have an ounce and a half in two different baggies, cause that's how I got it, and my scales are all in the living room in my coffee table drawer. It's all mine. Tonio doesn't even know I'm smoking because he is clean and doing good on paper, and he will leave if he finds out! Please, no, DONT RUIN MY FAMILY." I almost believed the lie myself. I told them my OBGYN was aware that I smoked and that all my children were healthy, and that is actually true. I have very intelligent children, and my doctor said it was fine for the baby, just relaxing. The agent asked why there was so much cash in our safe that they busted into before we got back. I said if you look under it you will see our recent tax return we just got back and the amount. He just looked at me with disgust and took me in the living room where there were people I didn't realize were in my house. I recognized my nephew Zachary's uncle Jessie and Zachary who was spending the night. Jessie, who was my buddy and my age, would stop in every now and then and I would hook him up. So tonight, I guess should have been no different. When I came into the living room, I saw Jessie and I saw a girl his age and an old man. I had never met him and I was thinking he set me up at first sight (because I was not thinking clear at all). Then I saw that they were all cuffed.

Jessie later told me he thought it was weird that Tonio was in the garage with a paintball gun. That laser definitely did not shoot paintballs. There were at least thirty agents in all black with huge guns scanning our eyes and every Springfield available unit. They called my mom home, they said to watch the kids and I was trying to console my sleepy babies and nieces, while cuffed, Zachary was helping me. The agent asked why Jessie was there and he said to pick up his nephew. The agent asked me why he was there. I said he was supposed to pick him up and take him to see his dad. When I tell you we had no knowledge of being questioned and basically said the same thing, that was God protecting us. I believe that it happens often.

I was sitting there watching the clock. It was 11:25. Antonio walked in at about 11:37 give or take a few minutes. I was so terrified because I knew how they treated me, Twila and her boyfriend. Let's face it: Tonio was black, he was already on paper, so I was so worried, that's why I was pushing that he didn't know anything about it so much before he got there. The moment he arrived, they immediately jumped on Tonio and took him to the ground. I think they searched him outside.

Then they took him into our bedroom and questioned him. By that time my momma had come home in an emergency to keep the girls because I assumed me and Tonio were going to jail. Nope, when Momma got there, they immediately arrested her for having half a Xanax and valium in her bedside drawer. They cuffed her and put her in the paddy wagon first (it was a transport bus). My momma had never had a speeding ticket and there she was going to jail. Hey, I never said she was an innocent lady, and wasn't culpable. I'm just saying, it was my momma. It broke my heart. The agent came out with Tonio. He asked me to stand up, so I did. The officer said, "We are not taking him?" He said, "Nope, just her and the mom." Me and Momma went to jail together. Tonio met us down there and bonded both of us out of jail immediately. We went back to the house and moved the fuck out right then that night and day. It was forever referred to as the crack house by my momma.

We got a paid lawyer the very next day. Tonio paid him $1,500 retainer until we knew what the charges were going to be. His parole officer told him he had to move out because I had a pending case, the only way to stay together would be to get married. We loved each other and he didn't really propose to me. We were already living like a married couple so we figured we might as well get married. I told him I wanted the best we could afford. We had two weeks and I was going to make it happen, and I did. We had an amazing wedding. We both cried. All our close friends and family were there, the music was bumping. We had about forty to sixty or so guests, we danced, and it was more than I dreamed of, and we got a jacuzzi suite. The only person missing was Twila, she was still in prison.

Chapter Eleven

We were now twenty-five. It was summer, 2005, and we had a huge bounce house that Dan and Karen set up. Karen is Boston's sister and Dan is her husband. We would hang out all the time. We love having dinner parties and BBQ's. We had a 5ft pool in the back, so the kids were in heaven. Between the bounce house and the pool, they barely slept. We had so many birthday parties that summer. I was still pregnant and having my Keannah! Yes, another girl was on the way at the end of August.

We took a vacation to Branson for Fourth of July that year with Dan, Karen, and Austin, and Catherine, Boston and Janie'. We had fun. Then around the first of August we went canoeing, me and Tonio in a canoe. He couldn't swim by the way, but he did have a life jacket on, thank God. I was nine months pregnant. We were in the water five minutes, and we flipped the canoe. It was about 5 inches deep, but deep enough that he lost all his beer. The current carried it quick as shit. We had a good time, even though he lost his beer. It bummed them the whole trip. I just laughed and enjoyed swimming. I love water. Always have. I'm a Pisces.

Our marriage was going great. I loved calling him my husband. He also seemed to take his role as a husband more serious than just being my boyfriend/baby daddy. We were very committed and both of us seemed to like it.

Keannah was born August 30, 2005 at 10:15am by C-section. Since I had one with Kaleah, that was what my doctor chose for this induction. She was 7 lbs., 6oz and had a head full of black curly hair, except behind her left ear, it was all red. She was so beautiful. We were complete with our tribe of Draper girls. They were all so beautiful, beyond my wildest dreams. I never thought of myself as ugly. But I never thought I could bring three little girls into the world that were all so beautiful. We were truly blessed, but this also scared me three times more because I had 3 girls to keep protected, but I thought Tonio would always be there to help so we would be fine. My past had been traumatic enough. I was starting to think about God, started to talk to him and thank him for everything for my family.

It was January 2006 and I got word from CeCe's mom; it was a voicemail from her crying from the hospital that Nancey aka CeCe had died! I went straight to CeCe's mom's house and could not find her. The next day, the Springfield morgue called me. I had been listed as the contact to make decisions on what to do with her body! I was in complete shock. I couldn't find her mom, who was known to do her share of smoking crack and meth. CeCe had two babies. They were one and two years old, and I knew they were going to need a place to visit their momma one day. I told the morgue to give me a day or so. I didn't want her cremated. I would figure out services. First thing I did was find her momma at a dope house, or the alley rather, and we did a story with the newspaper asking for donations. A lot of people did not want to help because CeCe died in a car chase running from the cops. We would find out later she was also ten weeks pregnant with a third baby that would never make it into this world. But I started on the phone calling everywhere until I had enough to give her a proper service and burial.

There were maybe twenty people in attendance at her funeral and six of them were cops that brought her children's father over in handcuffs. I even reached out to Inez to help me fly out her sober aunt, because I needed a sound family member to at least help with CeCe's mom and me. I was completely overwhelmed plus it was nice to meet Aunt Dotty from Chicago. I paid Inez back with tax money I would receive a month later. The funeral went as well as it could, being a funeral and all. I remember we all went to her mom's and had a BBQ; it was January 5, 2006. It was like 70 degrees and sunny and beautiful, which is uncommon. As her mom's phone was ringing, the ringer played "CeCe Don't Fear the Reaper." I swear we all heard it. We asked her mom and she said CeCe had come to visit her at Christmas just a few weeks before. She put that as her ringtone. After laying CeCe to rest. I was emotionally exhausted. I remembered drinking and finally just letting go and crying my eyes out, thanking God I had gotten it accomplished!

It was March 2006, my birthday, and our one-year wedding anniversary. We got married the day after my birthday because we had 30 days to get married, and rather than break it up to the end of march, and his birthday was February 1, we just chose my birthday to do a huge celebration of us every year. It made sense at the time because we were going to be together forever—right? Well, we had a great vacation planned just for me and Tonio. Momma kept the girls. We were really enjoying ourselves and Momma called the hotel and said a detective came by to arrest me. I told Tonio, my case had caught up to me. But we still had our lawyer on retainer so I told Momma I would deal with them when we got back from our vacation.

We returned from our getaway and before I could even address the situation two detectives were at my door with a warrant for my arrest for 100 unpaid misdemeanor tickets for paraphernalia under 34.5 grams of marijuana, saying they just gave me a ticket that night and I didn't pay for it. Tonio paid $1,000.00 just to get me out that night. I told them I was calling my lawyer. My lawyer told them they could either arrest me and he would meet me down there and I would get right out, or they could leave and he would take care of my $100.00 ticket. So I told the detectives that while still on the phone with my lawyer. They said they would just leave. I hung up with my lawyer. On the way out the detective said to me, "I've just got a question and I will leave, Hannah: tell me where did you get the marijuana from?" I looked him in his eyes and said, "Her name is CeCe!" It wasn't CeCe, but how stupid did he think I was?

We started planning a huge Fourth of July vacation in March with three couples to rent a house on the lake. It was going to be $2500.00 split eight ways, so we were going to have a lot of planning for a 7-day trip to Osage Beach, MO, where I was born. We were all excited, planning and making sure everyone got to do what they wanted to do. Me and Tonio thought it best to even rent a car, because his nice old classic tricked out Cadillac was not for family trips. By this time I was working in health and life insurance and making $33.00 an hour, sometimes twice what Tonio was making—and yes, still selling pot on the side but major low key about it.

We went on vacation and had a blast. The girls were almost 1, 3 and 5. Kaleah surprised us by how much she just loved water. We went to the water park, and she went down the biggest, highest water slide, some of the adults wouldn't go on. Me and Tonio fought over him getting a keg of beer, only because he was spending a fortune on ice, and it still went bad anyway. He had to buy more beer even though we had a ton of alcohol. It cut into the money for my special restaurant I had been wanting to go to forever and we didn't end up getting to go until 2019. The other thing I wanted to do was drag our mattress outside while on ecstasy and make passionate love while under the stars, but he was not about it. My feelings were hurt. But for the most part we had a great family vacation.

When we were driving back to Springfield from Osage Beach on from our Fourth of July vacation, I had Tonio drive me by my family's cemetery in Platte, MO. My whole side of my dad's family was buried there. I even had a plot there, before Kitty sold everything. We turned on 64 HWY going east towards Bennet Springs. We drove down the road I last walked down crying when my stepmom kicked me out, because that was the very last time I had even been on this highway anywhere close to daddy's family land. We came up on the hill where I would see the old broken-down gas pumps and finely manicured yard and the big old red barn, and the walnut tree next to the old red barn. I wondered how grandma's roses were doing. I was getting excited. We pulled up and I asked Tonio to slow down and pull on in. I was in complete shock to discover it was literally a junkyard! There were broken-down cars and junk everywhere, no roses at all. I felt so sad for my dad. I felt very sorry for grandma and grandpa even though they were in heaven. It was an insult to what they had stood for, and the hard work! Most of all I felt sorry for my girls who would never know the beauty of what I knew.

Everything had died. I was ready to get a couple miles down to the cemetery to see dad. It had been six years since he died, and I had not been back, like I said. We traveled two miles to Platte cemetery, and I found his grave. I saw it had ten-point buck on it, which I loved, but then just "Husband of Katherine." I was sick to my stomach. We just left and I cried silently to myself while listening to music the rest of the way home.

My momma started having issues at her job. I also believe menopause or—even more likely—PTSD kicked off a nervous breakdown after a girl sliced herself up really bad, hitting main arteries in front of Momma, and Momma later had to clean up the blood by herself. The girl was stitched and stapled up but came back after a brief stay at a hospital much like one I had attended in my early teens, where my momma had worked for ten years. Nothing like this had happened before. This was a free-range facility, meaning the girls didn't have real behavior issues, just housing issues for the most part, or waiting to transition to be an adult. My momma was being her normal self when they brought the girl back. That's when Momma lost it and went into an adult psychiatric care inpatient hospital.

Me and Tonio had to attend his best buddy Steven's funeral. That was a shock. Me and Tonio had dealt with a lot of death and loss in our twenty-five years of life. We were drinking and playing spades one night and we had never spoke too much about Tonio's dad. All Tonio said was that he lived in the Sikeston area of Missouri.

It was late after midnight, and I talked him into looking his dad's phone number up on 411—that was information. I called since I was a professional on the phone anyway. I got a number and Tonio worked up the nerve to call him right then and there! Next thing, he was on the phone with his DAD! He told Tonio that he and his wife were going to drive up from Sikeston to Springfield right then. They were going to hang up and get dressed and they were on their way!

So we waited the five-to-six-hour drive and sure enough they showed up. We had stayed up with all excitement. I thought, *How cool, the girls are going to have a granddaddy. Tonio's dad must really care a lot to just drive up here like he did.* Nothing could prepare us for what he would tell me and Tonio. He sat us down and began to tell us he had a DNA test done years ago, and it came back negative. He would be there, but he was not his biological father. Tonio understood, but was like, "Dude you could have just said that on the phone. You made it a big, huge deal coming up here getting my whole family and kids involved." They parted that day on good terms, but Tonio had questions for his mother, and he had them that day!

Tonio started calling his mom nonstop that day. He wanted real answers from his mom about who his real father was and his mom did not want to talk about it. Tonio called his uncles and her brothers to ask what they knew, if anything, and finally his mom agreed to let him come pick her up to sit down at our house to talk. She came over and she told him the truth. She had been sleeping with her mother's husband and believed he was Tonio's actual father, and he was dead and had been dead for many years. Tonio believed her and still believes that his step-grandfather, Mr. Draper is his actual father to this day. His family does too, at least the ones that I know. It was not something we discussed. It is just one of many reasons, and a big reason, I'm sure why our family got so fucked up.

CHAPTER TWELVE

Not long after that we were having a get-together in the back on the screened-in sun porch, playing cards and even had dominoes going and we were all drinking and having a great time. No fighting, just good music and tasty drinks flowing. Tonio was drinking his favorite cognac in a holiday glass. I know because out of nowhere all of a sudden, he just busted it over my head.

Before I could get my eyes open and wipe them from burning, I could hear his friends dragging him violently outside and he left for the night. Everyone was in shock! It was just like the time in the car, the night Cox saved me back in 2002. The next day Tonio was crying his eyes out saying he had no idea how it happened. He said the same thing that night too.

I was beside myself. I thought we were better, like all the way better, and would never see nothing like the evil monster hero again. But he had been me and the girls' hero for so long I couldn't understand what made him a monster and so violent for no reason! He said he had mixed way too much alcohol and took a hydro and he would never do that again. He promised. I let him come back home. I was so devoted to him, our family, our life. We had everything. Great jobs. We were still making side money on pot. Actually, we lost a pound of pot one night. We were drinking and one of us hid it and we couldn't find for weeks. Then all of a sudden Kaleah was like three years old and she came carrying it from the back bathroom. We still had no clue exactly where it was, but she brought it straight to me. At least she knew to bring it to me. Reminds me of myself. Not sure if that's good, but it is a fact.

My momma got out of the hospital on Social Security disability benefits and decided she wanted to live on her own in a little apartment instead of with constant kids all the time. Because we had our three girls and my oldest sister's four kids, Dylan, Sebrina, Zachary and Harley most weekends. Harley spent a lot of time with Terry. Him and my sister Heather split up a few years back, right after Harley was born. Because Momma got an apartment, we needed a place just a little cheaper.

It was just before Christmas 2006 and since we were moving, we didn't do our normal big festivals because we would be moving January 1, 2007, into a 2500 square foot duplex. But it seemed like a house. It was really cool. It had a master bedroom with a giant garden tub in the middle of the floor. The walk-in closet had a toilet.

Tonio did not condone shitting around his clothes, but it had an amazing master bedroom and two more big bedrooms upstairs and a nice living room and huge bathroom. And in the finished basement were two more living rooms and three more bedrooms. It was concrete, but it was finished with sheet rock and seemed perfect with a huge kitchen for me to cook my favorite food for my family. I loved to cook for Tonio and the girls and all our friends.

It was so nice hearing compliments. I was known for my barbecue seafood boils, fried shrimp, catfish, Applewood pot roast and homemade fried chicken, fried pickles, homemade cashew chicken and of course, homemade potato salad and sweet tea! I would say my top two was potato salad and my pot roast. I could get anyone to visit if I told them that was on the menu! So we were living the dream.

Tonio and I even traded the Cadillac in for a nice new SUV. It was a 1999 beautiful blue Suburban. We owed 19,000.00 on it, but we were doing good and the sky was the limit. I was a top setter band and was getting a lot of praise at the insurance company I worked at. I even got 100% quality bonuses often and that was a huge deal.

There was definitely a lot more money in insurance than vacuums and maybe even water. I wouldn't bet on that. But still, insurance is big business and starting at the very bottom didn't bother me. I had always some-how just felt capable of doing whatever I want if I really wanted. At 25, this was no different.

I wasn't born privileged, but I was born with a hell of a brain to communicate. At this point, I had learned very well how to sell or be sold, and that one or another is always going on in any situation, especially pertaining to money! So I was dedicated to my job or career. Tonio had been with his company for over three years and was a certified forklift driver with a great insurance benefit package at his job.

It was January 12, 2007 when the ice storm hit Springfield, Missouri. It was out of nowhere and extremely scary because over 90% of our area lost power. Some were out for three weeks. At the time we had a cell phone. They were just becoming affordable for everyone to have one. But we had the plan with after 09:00 pm and on the weekends, it was free and texting was not a big thing at all. We did lose power for maybe four hours and then it just came on and I turned our heat up and told Tonio to let everyone know we had room, and if their power didn't come back on and they didn't want to get a hotel to bring food and pillows and blankets. The next day we still had power and heat and I figured out how to send a multigroup message to everyone in the phonebook because yes, we shared the phone. That's what we did back then. I don't think life would be the same without technology.

We received so many replies and welcomed everyone and said, "Bring everything you got for survival. Foodwise, extra dishes, blankets, everything!" We had heard the grocery stores were blacked out and were throwing out perishables. We didn't even try to go to the store. The first thing we did was take a head count and see what all we had.

We had just received our tax return and it was around $10,000, so we were stocked up and with everything. We were okay even though there were at least fifty-five of us, mostly kids. God had given us a huge five-bedroom, three living room, two level, 2500 square foot home to get through this disaster together. We ended up smoking a whole pound of weed during the 14-day period before everyone was able to finally go home. We had just got it. Everyone we sold to was in a disaster living with us.

What were we going to do with everyone under one roof? One of Tonio's buddies that came brought his six-person hookah. We would go in the walk-in closet in the master bedroom at night because it would fill the whole upstairs with marijuana smoke. We had a lot of fun. Feeding time was on the clock and took all of us to cook for all the kids. Then adults eat according to pregnant females, to males. We got through it. That's all that mattered. My oldest sister was working for *The News Leader*, the local newspaper, and sent them to do a story on us. It was called "Draper Family Turns Home into Shelter for Friends and Family."

I was proud of that. I loved that Tonio was never jealous and wasn't ever insecure with me. He trusted me that way and never even tried to ask me to stop talking to any of my homeboys. They could come chill even while he was at work and drink a beer or blow a blunt. Like Orlando, he definitely used to show up and Marlin back in the day before he got locked up. Eric was like a brother. He was my neighbor and Orlando's best friend. He even had red hair. His Momma was amazing. I loved Ms. Donna. She called me her daughter. Ms. Donna was fun. I liked hanging out with her.

It was spring 2007 and Twila had just gotten paroled out to our house. She had been in prison since our house got kicked in and they rolled her back for absconding from parole. She started dating Boston the night she came home. We were all catching up. It was like the good old days, except me and Tonio were balling legally more than anything. We even had his favorite little cousin that was fourteen staying with us. Vashaun, Tonio's little cousin came to live with us. We wanted to try to give him a better life that what he had been going through. He parents at the time were struggling to keep a roof over his head. He was already on some Knucklehead Street shit, but he was my little dude and he was so helpful.

He was funny. He used to perform songs, lip syncing, or he would really sing. He was actually pretty good. Very talented. Vashaun had a smile that can light up any room. He also loved ramen noodles so much. I used to tell him, "Cuz, we don't got to live like that. We can get something really yummy like pizza rolls or burritos for a snack." But he loved his noodles. He was my little cuz. I really liked having him live with us.

We planned a camping trip for the Memorial Day weekend. We bought tents and everything you needed to go camping, and I had invited one of Kayden's little brother's mom with us. We had gotten really close over the years. He was the same age as Kaleah and so we all took off towards the Branson area and found a camping place that was nice and set up camp.

We had brought two cases of beer and a fifth of hard liquor. I remember Tonio started being rude about Kayden's brother's mom being there and I started telling him to stop and apologize to her, and the next thing I knew he was punching me. Vashaun jumped in and wouldn't let him keep hitting me! Me and my friend went into the kid's tent and I laid there and cried till daylight, when I was sober. I'm not sure how much I slept or if I did, but she was actually pregnant so we just left them there and took her car home.

I looked in the mirror when I got home and I had a huge black eye. I was so completely ashamed. I worked as a professional! How is this my life? My depression hit hard.

Tonio made it back from the campsite eventually with his crying bullshit. Once again, I told him I was done! He started telling me he would quit drinking. He promised he would never touch alcohol again because he never wanted to ever hurt me again. He swore. "Please Hannah." He said I meant everything to him. Could he just sleep on the floor at the foot of the bed? I was laying there so furious once again that this is where we were and this time the kids were actually involved. I felt so angry and bitter. I was also considering what he had said about getting sober and that we would only smoke pot.

He even said he would go to part-time work and take more time for us because money wasn't an issue.

I was thinking we had never in almost seven years had a real fight without crack, meth or alcohol involved. The only time we fought over pot was because he laced our last blunt on his birthday with coke and I refused to smoke it and I was pissed and left his ass in Branson. That was his 21st birthday. I took him to a resort and left him there over him lacing that blunt. Then I came back and bought all weed I could find. I was spiteful like that. You ain't going to fuck me over or disrespect me. So when he got back to Springfield, he had to get pot from me if he wanted some, and he did. We made up. Obviously, he knew he was fucking with a real one and I stood on my word.

So with his word that he would never ever drink again, I gave him one more chance. I was still at Seton making it in the insurance business. Tonio ended up taking a leave of absence from work because I was making so much money, we could afford it with no problem, and my big boss was coming down every week or giving his season seat tickets he wasn't using that week, so complimenting me on my performance. I had also been awarded the Quality of the Year award for 2006 and was well on my way for 2007. Being the employee with the best quality in the appointment setting for insurance agents was the highest compliment. It was way better than having a bunch of appointments that were no shows. Quality is always better than quantity.

The branch manager told me he was recording my calls and using them to get contracts in different areas down in Florida and that he would pay for me to get my agent's license. He said that I would make a quarter of a million my first year and he would even provide the books I would need. I thought, *Wow, he really believes in me, and I do too.* This became my dream, with Tonio home all the time that summer and me clearing well over $3,000 a week. I was having to work 08:00 am to 01:00 pm.

We had all kinds of what we called Draper Family Fun and every Sunday was Draper Family Fun Day. We were also having some small fights. Like one time I asked Tonio to go flip the breaker. He replied with something rude as hell and we didn't talk for a few hours over it. He later told me he didn't know what it was I asking him to do. That never occurred to me. But why was that my problem? I thought I did not deserve for him to be rude to me and I told him, "Next time just say you don't know." There is a lot I don't know that I got to figure out. I have never seen shame in asking for help or to learn how to do something I need to figure out. Daddy always said, the only thing you will get in this world for free is an education.

We were taking the girls' Jeep and wagon to the park almost daily and cooking out every chance we could, swimming at Momma's pool at her apartment complex, and really just having a calm summer. Tonio decided it was time to go back to work. Our duplex was leaking in the basement and it had black mold and was very unsafe, so we needed to move fast. Tonio had done really well with stopping drinking.

We found what I thought was the perfect house. It was literally right off 65 highway and Sunshine in Springfield. It was close to Tonio's job it was like a log cabin with a huge yard. It had brand-new carpet throughout. I loved that it had a three-level backed deck. The rooms were small but two bathrooms, a double garage, and a huge lot next to the house for the girls to ride their bikes and their Jeep powerwheel.

It was pretty, it even had a loft over the living room like a library. We moved in August 1, 2007. I had started praying that God would keep my family safe and bring us closer to Him. Vashaun told me they heard me praying out loud for God to protect our family and bring us closer to Him.

Before we got sober, however, we moved into our new house and I was busy making it ours. Vashaun got into some trouble with Juvey after beating up a kid for calling his little cousin a racist word. He ended up going to Sikeston and stayed with his momma. He was on that knucklehead shit. He got in some more trouble now that we lived way closer to Tonio's job.

He was coming home later and later all the time, every night, 30 minutes more. Since we had moved really close to Tonio's job I found it very strange that he seemed to be coming home quite a bit later than when we had lived all the way across town. And to top it off now, we constantly had gum in the truck. We never chewed gum before to this degree. I point blank asked him, "Are you drinking again?" He said, "No, Hannah baby, I'm not, really. Just a few of us been shooting the shit in the parking lot after work." I let it be. After all, he had not been drunk that I knew for sure. He did come home within a good hour from work, not drunk. I wanted to believe God was working on our marriage and I knew he was because right after we moved in the local Baptist church. He sent Brother John to our house to invite our family to church and the kids started attending Sunday school. They would ride the church bus. My niece and nephews would also go with them.

Chapter Thirteen

I will never forget Brother John. He was sent from God above! Brother John knocked on the door and wanted the girls to go to Sunday school, and I thought that was right on time and said, "Yes, of course." I wanted my kids to grow up in the Church like I did. I was constantly asking Tonio to go to church, I told him I thought it would be good for us to go and check it out.

He kept blowing me off. He will tell you this himself to this day. God wanted us then and he would demand our full attention! Even though I am not religious, I am extremely spiritual. I believe in God and that Jesus died for me and they both protect me. Always have and always will. I feel very highly favored and truly blessed in Jesus' name! Amen.

It was October 6, 2007. Tonio had been out all night. He came in. We had been fighting, I think for a few days. He may have even been gone longer. It's kind of a blur. But he came home and the girls was at my mom's. I do remember that he came in and went to the bedroom to lay down and ignored me. I was yelling at him, "Have you been drinking?" He jumped up and screamed at me, "Yes, you stupid bitch! You're a dumb bitch for even thinking I would really quit." I said, "Okay, I got your stupid bitch."

I went and took all of our family and wedding pictures off the shelves and walls and went in the bedroom and stood at the end of our cherry wood sleigh bed, my dream bed I bought, while he was laying there. I busted and tore all the pictures up and told him he had no family, that I was moving with the girls to the Florida office and I would be leaving soon. He said he didn't give a fuck and to leave him alone! I went to my momma's and just cried on her bed while the kids played because we had all my sister's kids between me and Momma.

My oldest sister in September 2007 sat all four of her kids down in my living room and told me and her children she did not want to be a mom; it was not rewarding and she was sending Harley to Texas to live with her dad. Sebrina would live with me, and the boys would live with Momma, and she was going to have fun with her new boyfriend. We will call him Peewee. Peewee was a tattoo artist and so far prior to this, Harley was the only kid Peewee would allow at his house, and he would draw on her with Sharpies. I didn't like him.

They actually both worked at my job for a few weeks but couldn't hack it, so my sister was telling her kids she was abandoning them basically and she didn't love them at all! She told them Aunt Hannah and Uncle Tonio would take care of them and she left them. I was in complete shock. Could it be another evil monster hero because she was my hero? When I was so little, I thought my oldest sister was so pretty and so badass.

I always won on who had the cooler older sister. The clothes she wore and her hair was the best 80s hair-band setup you ever saw, with a black trench coat and she didn't take no shit. She loved headbanging music and thrash metal. I really thought she was amazing, but now she had done some already very questionable things as a mom that she never witnessed from our Momma. She would put the kids to bed without dinner a lot and was just very harsh on Sebrina, who was such a sweet, kind girl. It was hard to watch the way my sister treated Sebrina. I always thought it had something to do with the seven and a half months she missed. But I would see my sister's evil hit a whole new low later on with me, then her kids and all of us.

I woke up at my Momma's and got Sebrina, Kayden, Kaleah and, Keannah and we went home. Me and Tonio didn't speak at all. I had nothing to say to him. October 6 was a Saturday so I would say that the following Tuesday Tonio told me I deserved to go out, and to pick anytime when he was off and go have fun, that I deserved it. So I called a girl that was married to a guy Tonio worked with and the same shift and her name was Tricia. Me and Tricia decided we would go out after her husband and Tonio got home from work on Friday evening, around 11:45 or 12:00 am. But the afterparty is always open till 06:00 am.

So no biggie. I told Tonio our plans. He didn't seem to have a problem. It was Friday night. Tricia was over. We were getting ready together like females do. I hadn't drank since May at the camping trip so I was taking baby sips, but sipping no less. It was probably close to 12 am when Tonio and Boston walked in from work with quite a bit of alcohol and he acted cool and gave me some extra money and we kissed and me and Trisha left. We went to the club till it closed at 1:30 am, then the after party till about 2:30. Then we got roast beef sandwiches at a 24-hour fast-food restaurant and went back to my house. We got there and Trisha got mad because her liquor she left was gone and she was really pissed off and threw her sandwiches and left angry and I could just feel the negative energy in the air. I remember thinking, *Fuck this, I'm going to bed. If he wants sex he will wake me up. We had been seven years.*

I was asleep by probably 3:30 am. Around 5:00 am I was awakened to wetness all over my face and head and the taste and smell of gasoline. I thought I swallowed some gas and I got my eyes open as quick as possible to figure out what exactly just happened. Where did gas come from? I saw Tonio standing at the end of the bed on the left end with a red gas can exactly where I stood destroying our pictures. His eyes were big, hollow and evil. He said, "Now you're going to fucking die bitch."

The best way to explain what happened next is I heard the sound the barbecue pit makes. That's how me and my bed went up in flames and it made that sound. That sound is a feeling for me. I had been asleep on my right side and I grabbed our huge king-sized down comforter engulfed in flames off me. But our room was small and it landed in the closet and my babies were asleep. Keannah and Kaleah's bedroom was on the other side.

I'm yelling, "Put the fucking fire out!" I was in flames. I didn't have enough room to do anything but rub my hands all over my body up and down. I was running. My hands were rubbing the fire out on my body. I ran to get pitchers of water, and the box in the room was still on fire. If the closet was still on fire, Tonio's clothes were close, too close, and could catch fire in the kid's room. I woke Boston up. He was asleep on the couch. "Help, help!" I screamed. "Tonio set me on fire. It's on fire! Help Boston! The kids!"

My niece Sebrina told me later that she woke up that morning and saw me all burned and that I told her to go back in the room and be quiet and not to wake the girls and that help would be coming. She told me she she did exactly what I asked her to and she also began to pray to God that he would let her take my place. Hearing my niece that was only 11 years old say that broke my heart. I told her, "Oh baby girl, I would never want that and God had me the whole time. I hugged her so tight. That morning, I remember just being in complete shock.

When Tonio came into the living room and just looked me in the eyes, his were black and hollow. I did say, "You have to take me to the hospital! I will tell them it was an accident!" He didn't say anything, he just walked back down the hall. I ran out the house to my next-door neighbor's house, banging on her door. That poor lady. What a sight I must have been that early in the morning. It was still dark when I knocked on her door. She answered and said, "Oh please don't wake my grandbabies." as she handed me her cordless phone with 911 already dialed. I looked just awful and I completely understand she didn't want the grandbabies seeing me how I looked. I met her granddaughter years later and she did remember me that morning and she told me I had left stained black smoke on her grandmother's white cordless phone. it must have been very scary to her and all included, I'm sure. It's certainly not common that someone gets set on fire and knocks on your door at 5ish am for help. She told me when I met her years later that she was so glad I made it through that. They were doing God's work.

I was on the phone with 911 just praying, "Jesus let me hear sirens." I then saw Tonio come out first in our truck and leave. It was getting to be daylight now. Not long after that I saw Boston come out and get in his car and leave. I was telling 911 everything and constantly praying to Jesus to hear sirens. All my kids were in the house alone. "Please Jesus, let me hear sirens." And finally, I heard the firetrucks and ambulances coming and knew everything would be okay.

They were putting me in the ambulance and I remember saying, "Antonio Lamar Draper, 1 February

1981, Blue 99 Suburban," and then I fell asleep. I don't remember waking up for six and a half weeks in the burn ICU with 28% chance to live, burned 67%. But there were visits. I kind of remember some and some I don't. The doctors had me in a medically induced coma for my safety. I also had to have multiple surgeries, and that meant skin grafting. I would be able to wake up and stay awake. The first week of October I would wake up on a metal table naked with bandages of all kinds, with people all around me and I could smell cow shit. I had no idea what was going on, but soon I would be back out again.

The day they woke me up, I kept asking for Tonio and my momma. They wouldn't really reply to me, and I wanted my husband. They started asking me questions. Then soon the prosecutor for the case was in my burn ICU room to question me. After being awake a few hours, I could remember enough. I knew I saw Tonio with a gas can and a blanket on fire in the closet and waking up Boston and telling him to get water and praying. I remember praying. "Where are my kids? Where are they? Are they OK?" They told me they were fine and with my mom, and the ICU had special visiting hours. My mother would be up later. I thought they were all lying to me. I looked out the window because I got moved to the burn unit. That just means you're not behind glass facing the nurse's desk. I was ready to start seeing how my grafts would do and to hopefully not get an infection, because that is what the doctors said was the actual high risk, and I needed to consume as many calories as possible and stay very clean.

I had 05:00 am mandatory head-to-toe scrubbing since I was burned 67%. I had pig skin put on my back. I couldn't wiggle my toe. I was angry! I wanted to leave! I didn't believe it was that bad at all. I truly thought they were lying! I thought they were holding me hostage. I was in Salem, Missouri. I had been there when I was 13 or 14 and met some devil worshippers, and I thought they had come to get me and everything was a lie. I didn't believe I was in St. John's Catholic Hospital where all three of my girls had been born. Even looking out the window looked foreign. My oldest sister came up there with Pewee and I was scared, and he jumped off my bed to scare me more. He liked whatever I was going through. Evil people are like that. This lasted the first couple days.

Then more people that I knew in Springfield came to see me. I will never forget how I felt the first time I woke up and had access to a phone before any visits and I wasn't strapped down. There was one on my hospital bed the whole time, but I was very sneaky and I could only remember one number. It was Inez's number, so I was quiet as can be, and I dialed her number, hoping she would answer and send the police to come save me quick! It rang and rang and she answered and I whispered, "It's me, Hannah. I need help!" She yelled, "You're awake?" I was like, "Shush, they will hear us." She said, "Hannah, you're in the hospital." I told her,

"Yeah, that's what they keep saying. But it seems weird." She told me she loved me and would visit me as soon as they let her. She did. Her mom, or as we called her, Grandma, was in the same hospital in ICU, battling emphysema. Twila was still in prison; she didn't get released until 11-17-2007 and she finally completed her prison sentence and was off parole.

It took me four days to walk with a safety belt, but I was good to go to the surgery floor soon. That meant I could maybe move around the hospital and go to the beautiful chapel in St. John's. Oh, I must tell you about my favorite nurse. Well, she was a certified nursing assistant, but she was an angel in the burn unit. She would come in with them. Sometimes the CNAs would come in just grabbing at you, ripping your bandages, and I would scream, "What the fuck? Leave me the fuck alone. What the fuck?" And she would say so sweetly in her Hispanic voice, "Oh no this is a Christian hospital, we say what the fudge!" So when she was on duty, I would respect her. Later, I asked all of them to forgive me. I was really messed up.

The burn unit was very scary and painful. Whether you went to the tank or they did it in your bed depended how much and where your burn and donor spots were. I went to the tank, where they stripped me down in a ten-foot by four-foot-deep tank, and I was in a holster and slowly lowered me into the tank, but only to my waist. I would be freezing and screaming from the pain. It was pure torture. Then I would lay on a metal table naked while they rebandaged me every morning. I did get a new normal about three weeks after being awake, and I could now do pretty well with a walker. I would even get out the burn unit, and they would let me go to the chapel or cafeteria or look at gifts in the gift shops and even go outside for fresh air. I would get anyone I could up there every chance I could to take me in a wheelchair to smoke a cigarette.

One day the nurse said, "Ms. Kendrick, if you're going to completely defy doctor's orders, will you at least smoke on the north lawn where we can't see you?" I said, "Yes, ma'am. No problem." They understood I was completely broken and half dead inside emotionally, and the half that was alive was fucking angry.

The first day the prosecutor came and saw me, she told me Tonio was going to get sixty years. She asked me what Boston's involvement was, possibly to charge him. Boston had nothing to do with what Tonio did to me. The next official person that in wanted to know where the Suburban was, and I didn't know! I yelled, "Bitch, are you serious? I've been in the fucking hospital over two months. Get the fuck out my room!" Then a DFS lady came in with her clipboard and said my kids would stay in custody until I could physically take care of them myself, and that would be seven to nine months. They were with my mother until she got sick, she fell asleep in the chair while the DFS lady was visiting the kids. Then they were immediately, physically taken into custody. I was fucking mad. Are these people insane? My kids. What? It was the worst day of my life!

I also looked in the mirror that day. These crime scene photos give the best idea of what I saw. I looked like something blew up in my face. I would not wish what I went through on anyone but sex offenders. I'm brutally honest. I don't sugarcoat shit, never have, never will. And I love hard! So my arms were melted in kind of like a chicken wing. Normal people have zero range. I had zero range. I had 90 in in one and 70 in the other. But I was ready to go home.

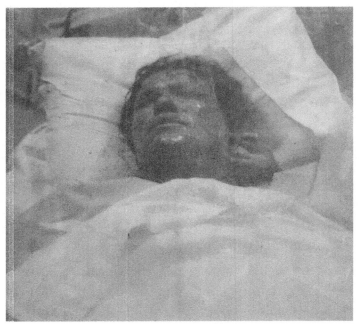

Photo: Hannah Kendrick

Chapter Fourteen

I heard my oldest sister was collecting money on behalf of me and my kids. The church Brother John was from had raised a few thousand and my sister spent it before I had even woken up from my coma. I was calling my house phone telling her I was getting out and would be home the Wednesday before Thanksgiving, and she didn't believe me. And now that my Momma had to take my kids, my sister was forced to take her kids back and proceeded to take over my house and basically moved me out. She told me she figured I didn't want to live there.

I told her I would be there Wednesday and I wanted my house back for Thanksgiving. My momma had come to me at the hospital with a staff to help me fill out disability paperwork and I said, "I don't need that. I can still fucking work. I have my voice. I'm fine." I thought I was anyway. I had no idea how much anger would control me for the next eleven years. They tried to get me to file for disability in the hospital and I told them absolutely not, I was not disabled and I was going back to work as soon as possible, so I denied applying for disability.

When I came home that Wednesday in 2007, before Thanksgiving, I was not prepared for my momma to pull me into my driveway and seeing my sister was having a yard sale with all my stuff. There was a man in a S-10 pickup backed up to my door. He had my deep freezer loaded and I was struggling straight out of the hospital with my walker leaning up against his truck. He says, "I gave her $30 for it." I start telling him, "No, this is my stuff. My husband just set me on fire! I'm just now getting out the hospital." My sister yelled at him and said, "Just go on ahead. She doesn't know what she is talking about. She suffered brain damage."

I had already told Momma to call the cops on this crazy bitch. She had officially lost her whole fucking mind. She got $2500.00 from the church and my utilities were ready to be shut off. I was home long enough to see Heather destroy my house and have Thanksgiving with my kids, who were staying with friends. Jackie and Tommy came, and Gina, of course my momma came, and even DJ, Eric and Tori and Nancy, Mr. George, Gina and Christina's dad and my closest friends. It all turned to a blur because later on that night I started having severe pain in my mouth and ended up back in the hospital with an infection. I was in there until the week before Christmas 2007. I hated the hospital. I had the worst experiences there.

The Hospital: Dreams or Spiritual Warfare

They said it was the morphine, but it was the devil trying to take me by fear that would never work. It would
happen in my dreams mostly but felt extremely real to
me! I would not be burned at all, and they would have
me strapped down for no reason. And I had a baby, but
they wouldn't let me see my baby. They told me it was
half-goat, and I was chosen. I was special in that they
would take the baby to the farm to get fed because I
wouldn't be able to feed.

Because I was a human, although a very special chosen one who would be taken care of, everyone would
smile and praise me. Even my Momma. She was smiling so big and she was so proud of me. It was so weird.

I kept saying, "I want to see my baby!" All I knew
was it was a girl and half-goat. It felt evil in my room.
And why did I have to be strapped down? I didn't
understand.

Nothing was wrong with me at all. No burns, but I
felt hot and sweaty from crying. Soon I was still completely alone in my very plain hospital room. It actually
looked like just a white plain room with nothing on the
walls at all, just a window on the right. But it faced a red
brick building.

Nothing to see at all. All of a sudden, a tall, dark-head-
ed man with dark brown eyes, with no facial expression
except cold and hollow, sat on the side of my bed, and

he leaned his body away from me towards the corner as if he was sharpening something. I was tied down. Still, I felt his negative evil vibes, and I also think he had a dagger that he was sharpening, but I couldn't see it and he looked me in my eyes and said, "It's okay. All the pain you're going through is making Satan stronger." I screamed at him, "I AM GOD'S CHILD! YOU CAN NOT BE HERE! GET OUT, I'M GOD'S CHILD, I AM GOD'S CHILD, GET OUT YOU CANNOT BE HERE, I AM GOD'S CHILD," over and over and he got out.

There was another time when I dreamed that I wasn't burned at all. I was an adult at my old family home in town in Buffalo, and there was a party going on and Jesse showed up. He had been in an explosion and he was badly burned. I told him I knew where to take him. We would go to St. John's Hospital in Springfield, to the burn unit. It was instinct. Even though I had not been burned in my dream, I just needed to get all these people out of my house and I would take him and they wouldn't leave. They were like zombies or tweakers just ignoring me. None of them would make eye contact with me and all of a sudden there was a huge white six-foot, nine-inch bald man. He was staring me down, straight into my eyes, getting closer and closer, smiling. I began to scream, "YOU HAVE TO LEAVE, YOU CAN'T BE HERE. I AM GOD'S CHILD!" He just laughed really loud with his nose almost touching mine. I repeated, "YOU CAN'T BE HERE, I AM GOD'S CHILD," over and over until I woke up in my hospital bed. I was completely drenched in sweat, my whole body.

Even my bedding had to be changed and some of my bandages. I ran out of my hospital room. It was my second stay. I could walk fine again, but I ran to the nurse's desk screaming for a priest or a nun, anyone, please come pray with me right now. A nun came very soon.

I explained everything I had endured and what just happened in my dream. She told me it sounded like spiritual warfare and I was doing exactly what I needed to do and to continue. The devil would leave me alone, and we prayed after. She explained that I felt better and then I never really experienced anything like that again.

I got back out of the hospital a week before Christmas. My friends Eric, Laura and her baby daddy and DJ, his girlfriend at the time and Twila and my momma and my sister Roci was down from KC to help me for as long as I needed her and she was there to help me get my babies. They had taken them from my Momma for getting sick with pneumonia and falling asleep on a home visit. My poor Momma felt awful! I look back and it breaks my heart, but everyone was there to help me get my house back together from my oldest sister Heather destroying it. Momma was such a huge help.

The first real week I got out of the hospital, just before Christmas 2007, I would have to go to court and see Tonio. I had no understanding how I would react to seeing him in court. I still needed my walker for the most part. I did depend on it but felt able and free, and getting better every day. I got weak walking into the courtroom and was ashamed of what I looked like. I was completely covered, not wanting him to see. I had gone from 218 pounds to 126 pounds, was bald, and my face was chapped and rashed, like road rash healing. I had no idea how weak I would feel. I almost couldn't walk. I couldn't breathe.

The judge asked if I needed to take a break. I said no and proceeded to the stand. I could barely speak in the beginning but answered the questions the prosecutor was asking me. Like my name, my address, who Antonio Draper was. As I was answering the easiest questions in the world, I was getting enraged. I was staring at Tonio. I couldn't stop. I started having uncontrollable outbursts, but no one stopped me. They let me say whatever I wanted to him and when they were done and I was able to leave, I picked up my walker up and walked past him saying, "I should kick you in your face, you fucking bitch!" The whole time in court, Tonio was shackled with his head down mostly and was crying.

I left court that day feeling less of a victim, but I was not yet a complete survivor. That would take self-work, healing, faith, and most of all forgiveness and God himself. I had gotten extremely angry, especially after my oldest sister stole all the money from the church that was raised for my kids, and I made everyone leave me alone. I refused to let anyone in and had my door deadbolted and was taking care of myself. Roci had to go back to KC and get her stuff and I would not let anyone in! The next day I had bed and a Porta potty at the end of my bed in the living room.

Well, I was taking care of myself. I was a grown ass woman so I got up to go potty. No biggie. I had done it a few times by myself. Well, I slipped and hit my head on the fireplace and was too far from anything to pull myself up. I had no life alert bracelet, so I was laying there for about two hours before someone showed up, I don't even remember who. Momma and Brother John from the church had spare keys because we also changed my locks, but I wouldn't let anyone even come over for a day or so except Brother John. He would come every day and just read the Bible. He didn't care if I smoked cigarettes and I let him know now when I was going to smoke pot, because I did not want to disrespect him. It would be rude to have pot in God's worker's face if he minded. He would step outside and come back maybe fifteen minutes later if I wanted to talk. We usually did. If I didn't want to talk, or was throwing a fit, he just sat calmly reading his Bible. Brother John stayed a few weeks straight until we got the swing of things. A true godly man Brother John was.

I still pray him and his family. He was truly and angel sent by God.

Chapter Fifteen

We went to court a few days later, still before Christmas 2007. It was family court to see the judge about my girls. I had not seen them. The DFS lady was a complete bitch, and I had remembered she said, that I could not have my kids until I could cook and prepare their food for them. They were two, four and six years old.

My sister Roci, who had my oldest nephew, Alex, who was 13, said she would come and live with me and be my caretaker. She was very capable of taking care of her nieces! We got to the family courthouse. I was so nervous. I didn't want to seem weak, so I left my walker in the car. We got in there and they had metal chairs that sloped back. So now I was doubly nervous because my leg strength was so weak, I couldn't stand up alone at all. I was praying so hard. We got into court and the judge looked at my situation and asked the DFS team where my kids were and told them to get my kids back with their mother as soon as possible! He said, "How dare you even try to keep them away! The sister is a competent caretaker. I want them returned to

Ms. Kendrick immediately." That meant they would be home for Christmas. We were basically adopted by the whole town. Santa even delivered my kids, me and my momma bunch of presents.

My friend Angel, who I used to work with at the insurance company, took the girls to the mall to get new dresses, got their hair done and pictures made. They surprised me with a portrait of three different adorable poses. Angel is a great friend and mother of her own two girls today. We were very blessed with gifts from the community that year. We felt a lot of love and support.

I was now in the hospital for the third time. There was this one nurse I could not stand. He was so fucking happy all the time. He would come in my room bright eyed in the morning after my 5:00 am scrub. I always napped good, and here he would come opening my curtains, letting the sun in and getting on my nerves with his morning cheer and pure happy shit. I would try to get him to fuck off, but he would say, "Well, it is what it is," and "Oh Hannah, it could always be worse, don't say that." Ugh, then was just not the time every day, but looking back, it was exactly what I needed. I thank God for his sweet soul. I apologized to him several times for my ill tongue. I do have an ugly mouth on me sometimes. It's been an ongoing battle.

When I got out of the hospital, I could not go to work. I was still sick, but I had plans to return after my third set of surgeries where they released my arms that were at ninety- and seventy-degree radius. Where I was telling you yours were at zero, mine were stuck in like chicken wings. I learned how to do most things with my feet. Physical therapy was torture. She would place her knee on my upper arm and press my lower arm down firmly. It hurt extremely bad and I could not handle it stretching and popping, and if I was not wearing my full-length arm braces they would immediately draw up.

I would have people hold cigarettes for me. I would grab my phone and throw it at my face. I could answer it just fine, but it was not long before I just gave up on wearing the stupid braces on my arms. If this was my new normal, that was fine. I accepted that I was not going through any more pain.

I was going through enough emotionally. I filed for state cash assistance and got $392 for my family of four. Rent was $700 and Momma only got $650 in SSI. Utilities had not been paid since Inez paid them, and they were close to being shut off for $950 backpay plus a $500 balance. I called the old branch manager at the insurance company and they paid off my city utilities, the whole $1,450, and said I had a job.

So I tried, and I did it as a commission-only arrangement: you made an appointment, or you made nothing. I was there for three weeks and that's what I made! Nothing. I just left. Rather than sit there and just cry, I could at least take the state assistance of $392 and buy a half pound and flip it. And we would make rent and pay the utilities and keep our phone on and pay for the trash service and all the house supplies because we were a house full. Either Roci was taking care of me, or Twila or Aunt Trish. I was lying in bed watching the headline news 24/7 and selling pot from my bed. I only got up for money and for showers.

Twila kept the house clean and I kept the bills paid. I found a connection in Kansas City. Although he was staying in the Federal halfway house, he would meet me somewhere safe. He protected me. He was actually a really nice guy. He would give me a pound of pot and I would drive it back to Springfield and wire him his money back from his people that I delivered to that night by 09:00 pm. I did that three times a week for a couple months. Then it died out. Not really sure what ever happened.

Tree and his people showed back up around this time. The only one balling was Ol Bruh. He was the oldest and least likely to catch a female. He was also known to trick off for no reason, give away money and cars to girls. Well, he showed up and had a bunch of ecstasy and we all started partying and I realized it made me feel like stretching my arms. I start hanging from my door frames. This would go on. All of the summer of 2008 Ol Bruh and Twila got together and he would give us what was called a boat. It is a Mason jar full of ecstasy pills and we owed him $1 apiece and 3000 in a jar, so $3000 for him. They go for $20 apiece, so that's all profit. Not going to lie, we showed out and went to the strip club Tori was working at the time and threw all the pills on the stage and yelled out, "Everybody chase the rainbow." We were doing it big and being carefree. I needed to not think about my reality.

I started to stay home and do my ecstasy while Twila and Laura would go out and I would play music (my kids had always slept through loud music). I would take X in, hang from the door frames and just stretch. I would do it for hours. It felt good! I mean it really felt good to stretch my arms on X. So Twila and Laura would bring the club home with them and we would party all night. The activity in my neighborhood was obvious, but I had stopped taking X, stopped hustling pot and having stopped traffic at my house because I saw police driving by, and they never drove down my street.

I had even decided to go ahead and file for my disability. The end of July 2008, I completed my phone interview and I cried so hard the whole time. My dad had taught me that I was nothing if I didn't work for my family. I got my first SSA check in August 2008. That was amazing. I had heard horrible stories, but mine went straight through.

I was getting that feeling again. The creepy, surrounded feeling. I was completely clean. Nothing in my house for weeks. I was actually just buying personal small bags because I was tripping out on an old boy in KC. He just stopped all contact. But I was partying hard from February to June 2008. Maybe I was tripping. Maybe not. I will never forget, Momma was sitting on the couch doing her medicine for the week, putting them in her Sunday to Monday box like she did every week. Zachary, who was almost ten now, was staying over, but he, along with my three girls, who were almost three, five, and seven, were asleep in bed. It was around 09:00 pm or so when we heard what sounded like an army of men running up on the porch. I heard, "Springfield Police Department, open up!" as they proceeded and immediately hit my door with some kind of huge ramming tool and kept repeating the same thing as before.

By the third time I was almost to the door to unlock it and they knocked the whole frame out. "Springfield Police, get down!" I was trying. I was not completely healed at all. My arms were maybe 60/70, and my Momma couldn't get down. She was old and overweight. We complied. The agents in all black started coming in. It was like the older ones and new ones and the one in charge wanted to know where the fuck the guns and crack were. I looked at him like, *Are you fucking serious?* I told him, "Officer, you got the wrong person. I do not have and have not had or even been around crack or guns." I told him I had a red bong in my house if he was taking me to jail. Let's go! He told me, "I know you smoke crack. We all know you smoke crack." I said, "Okay, smart one, bring your CSI box in here and let's do UA (urinalysis), because you will find marijuana and everything I have a prescription for." They did not give me a UA, but they completely destroyed my house. My kids and nephew had to wake up so they could toss their rooms in. They had a female officer search me and even bend over and cough like when you get booked in jail.

The kids were just watching again as thirty or so agents and officers destroyed our house and talking so much shit while they did it. I mean, I get it. I had been a shitty mom partying a lot, but Momma had my girls and they were very well taken care of at all times. Their search came up with the red bong I had already told them about. They gave me a ticket. I paid $100 for their once again multi thousand-dollar cost bust. They had zero correct info. If they came looking for money, weed or X, then I would have thought they knew everything, but it was just way too much shitting where I sleep.

Chapter Sixteen

So I moved to Corinth, Mississippi, to be close to Amanda V and my nephew. Her old man was an asshole, but we needed a change and Corinth was going to be it. We moved October 2008. It was Amanda's town I had heard so much about. I got us a house. It was perfect at the end of a farm road. Two-story barn style. Beautiful. We were in the country with no one to bother us and, most important, no more agents ever tearing our house up again. So we lived in the country on the outside of Corinth in Alcorn County.

I had been to a lot of small towns and at first, I liked this one. It seemed OK. Amanda and her boyfriend and son had moved here in 2004 to get away from meth in Springfield and have a better life for their family. Funny how the devil is everywhere. I would find out soon. Her old man was cooking dope down and things had just gotten worse and we never got to hang out and visit. He would record and switch our words around that she just still wanted a black man. He was the only white dude she ever gave a real chance to. I had my girls and

Momma and we had what we needed. I was trying to escape my brain so I tried unpacking the house and really just moving in.

It was now January 2009 and we had a fresh start. Unpacking and painting the whole kitchen red, me and Momma got hooked on the fix your house up shows. I found three ecstasy pills in my stuff that had been missed. I took them. I didn't feel them. They must have gotten old and the effects did not work.

Some weeks passed and I was just getting more depressed. I was already abusing Xanax and I was on fentanyl pain patches. I didn't know about them except I changed them every 72 hours and there was always medicine leftover in the patch. My curiosity got the best of me and I cut my patch open instead of throwing it away, and I tasted it. It took me so high. Warm, calm, and completely relaxed and numb.

I could handle life feeling like this. All of a sudden, I had this craving for money and to buy stuff. I figured out me and Momma could both get payday loans and buy nice stuff we wanted and would pay them back. Then we could really see what Corinth was about, eat at the best restaurants, and see what they had in Good Ole Miss. We both got $500, but I came to a couple days later and I had a whole complete wardrobe. Five purses, four pairs of $100 dollar shoes, and clothes on top of clothes, all with tags. The kids also got a bunch of new stuff, even more than me. I found all these receipts in my purse and in all the bags and some in the car and trashcan, and I took almost everything back. I was even more depressed. Life had caught up to a deep hole and now I was only wearing the patch for two days at a time and soon I wasn't even putting it on. I was ignoring my kids and life. I just wanted to sleep.

I remember I called a friend who was in publishing and ran a small newspaper in Springfield. I called her. She hadn't heard from me since first getting out the hospital, meaning she didn't know I was completely fucked up. Besides, her idea of morning coffee was a coffee cup full of vodka and a splash of coffee for color—not judging. But I asked her if I wrote my story, would she help me? She replied, "Hannah, you need to get a happy ending." For all she knew I did. I mean, I didn't, but damn, I thought me living was the happy ending. But I would find recovery before I found my happiness because it has yet to end.

As I write this alone at 04:30 am on March 19, 2021, my daddy would have been sixty today. Happy birthday, my evil monster hero. Daddy, I know you stay with me every day until we meet again.

I got word from the prosecutor. They needed me to fly back to Springfield for my divorce and that way they could proceed with charges in case I had to testify if he took it to trial. They flew me from Tupelo, Mississippi to Springfield Regional Airport and put me in the Plaza Hotel for four days. I don't remember a lot of it, except I remember being in court about our divorce. They did not bring Tonio in for our divorce hearing, and everything was finalized without him. His rights were terminated, but he was also set to pay child support. Once released 30 days from prison, he is to pay $575 for both Kaleah and Keannah. His plea bargain he was taking was 20 years with 85% served. He wouldn't see the parole board for a long time, and he had a prior gun charge.

I had a homeboy hit me up and offered to take care of him. I said no, even though I was super mad. Him being dead was not going to do anything but hurt my children. My homeboy's never getting out. He got a couple life sentences. He protected us. It's hard to explain, but that was years later. So I flew back to Mississippi after court for a little bit before I decided we were going back to Springfield. It was around Easter, because when we came back, we stayed at Eric and his family's house, and I remember Easter dinner.

From Halloween 2008 to Easter 2009 we moved two times, and I was trying to move again into one place, which we found right by our last house in Springfield that I had gotten burned in. It was two streets over. Twila and her girls came to stay and she was taking care of the girls and me and my Momma was just living, watching me go on a spiral downhill with my medication. I hit an all-time low and talked Mom into getting a title loan. Not for drugs at all: I was addicted to shopping. I love to buy things. Pools, clothes, toys, you name it. I loved shopping, sleeping and partying.

Me and Twila were both taking my meds. They were my prescriptions. So my house was not hot at all, or so I thought. At first, I was selling a very small amount of pot just to smoke for free. They came one day to repossess a car for the title loan we didn't pay. I had just eaten a whole 75 mg patch of fentanyl and took maybe four bars of Xanax, and I was telling them no, I was holding on to the car. I really believed that I could keep them from pulling off from me holding on. Well, they did anyway. My adrenaline was pumping so fast I thought I was sober. I ate another 75 mg patch and 33 Xanax and 60 Restoril.

I overdosed! I woke up in ICU on a ventilator and they stabilized me and sent me as a suicide intent. They also put another patch on the inside of my left thigh. So when I got to the unit, I went in my bathroom, tore it open and ate it and went and sat in the day room high as hell. I had a guy visit me and bring me in a cigarette and lighter, which I kept inside me till I smoked my cigarette that was in my shoe.

Then I flushed the butt and held the lighter in my vagina for the rest of my 96 hours stay I had left. They smelled the cigarette and strip searched me and found nothing. They could not figure it out. Of course, I was guilty at this point.

I knew these things to be a fact. God had me. And I knew that because of a visit to the outpatient burn unit at St. John's in 2008. I met a little girl who had her hands burned, and it made me think of my hands I had used to put myself out with. I looked at my hands as they appeared flawless and without any scarring at all! I met other burn survivors while going for outpatient appointments for my follow up care and there was a trend. A lot of people suffered issues with their hands, because we all used them most likely to put ourselves out. And here I sat looking at what I now call my footprints in the sand. But I also knew I could not seem to die and go to heaven and leave this evil world that showed me very little happiness and so much evil. So I was reckless trying to get to God fast because I had always believed I was truly his. I just had to find my path! It would come in his time. I had more to learn to testify later to you. I started to get the feeling my house was being watched. I saw police start driving by randomly. We were not doing this again, so I immediately moved me and Momma and the girls to Bolivar, Missouri, where Cox was living and tattooing and working as a roofer. He wanted to take care of me and the girls. He also did not like seeing me the way I was on my meds. Me and Cox had been seeing each other, dating, I guess. We got a place together in Bolivar. We moved into two trailers, one for us and one for Momma. We were living good in the trailer park! He reminded me of the old days he was tattooing and making extra money staying in the trailer, but it would not be long before we would find we were really just better off as good friends. The romance was not there, but the friendship still is today.

I wasn't prepared for how bad the opiate epidemic was in Bolivar, and they knew exactly what my fentanyl was, probably more than me. The local pharmacists had gotten busted for illegally selling narcotics and other medications not long before I had moved there and it seemed the whole town was strung out bad. It was a small town, that neighbored Buffalo, actually. I became "Burned girl with the patches." I saw a girl with a patch on that I sold her. They were taken to the hospital. Thank God, she made it. I stopped selling them and I only ate them from then on. That was summer 2009. I lived in Bolivar till January 2010 and we moved back to Springfield and life would change dramatically again! But it would do it again in August that year before I would stop filling my patches and tell my doctors what I was doing. That was hard to do, but I would still have plenty of other medicine.

Towards the end of January 2010, my oldest sister was missing. Peewee's mother, Ingrid, called me and asked me if I had heard from her, and said the cops were looking for her. I told Ingrid I had not talked to my sister since I lived in Bolivar. Just after Christmas break when I had the kids, I asked her where the kids were and she said she left guardianship of Dylan, Sebrina, and Zachary to her, so she had them. Then she stumbled and said, Harley, who was seven at the time, the same age as Kaleah, was in foster care and she didn't know why. Ingrid told me Heather, my oldest sister who had four babies, just took off. I thought about what she did right before I got burned. Ingrid told me I could have visits if I wanted to. I was thinking, *Visits, you're damn right. I'm also going to figure out what the fuck is going on!*

The kids came the following weekend to stay. Me and Momma went to grab groceries to feed all six of the children. We were in a five-seater car so we left the kids at the house and me and Momma ran to the store to get food for all eight of us for the weekend. We were leaving the store when, all of a sudden, the US Marshalls jumped out, calling me Heather, my sister's name. I was in pure shock! I said, "No, I'm Hannah. Can I help you?" Heather had been missing a few weeks now. The US Marshall told me he was looking for Peewee. He wouldn't tell me anything else. He let me and my Momma leave the grocery store and return home to the kids. Not long after we get home, there was a loud knock at the door and I went to answer it. We had just moved in. No one knew where we lived but Ingrid, who dropped off the kids earlier. The same agent from the grocery store was at my house. He said he got a Crimestoppers tip I was hiding Peewee. I said fuck no. He had my house searched and said Pewee was wanted for first-degree child molestation and my sister was with him, voluntarily it appeared! I asked him, "What about my niece? What about my other niece and nephews and Ingrid?" He told me those were questions for Family Services. He was a federal agent.

I didn't know what to do. Ingrid came and I let the kids go that Sunday evening, but I let my niece and nephews know before they left that I was going to fig-ure out exactly what was going on and I would be there to get them as soon as I had a chance and knew I could legally. By now I was actually clean except for smoking weed. I was just chilling. I had enough bad medical side effects and seizures and memory issues and a new money shopping issue, but I was doing a little better.

I called the police station the next day to find out what is going on. I needed to see what rights I had to my nieces and nephews. And how was Harley? Where was she? It took forever, but I got the lead detective on the phone and he told me that if he was me, he would go get his nephews and niece from Ingrid, that I had every right as their aunt. He told me Harley's dad was on his way from Texas to get her and he, the detective, would keep me updated. He told me it was a first-degree child molestation case and my sister and Peewee were wanted. He was not sure what part my sister played because she was originally arrested for property damage, but now it appears she had left with him. It was about four days later when the US Marshals caught my sister and Peewee together in Utah. Because of that, I did a sneak pickup of Dylan, Sebrina and Zachary from each of their schools and took them by Ingrid's to get stuff very quickly. With the lack of clothing they had, we had to get them stuff, so we did what we had to do. Dylan was fifteen, not a little kid anymore. He remembered where a fire extinguisher was, so we went to go get it because we did not have $50, so he got it for free for us. Sebrina said, "Are we stealing?" I said, "We are doing what we have to stay together." All I wanted was to keep us together. We would keep empty food boxes in the pantry and Momma would write bad checks every day or so when we were low or out of food for pizza because we were out of money. The kids got so sick of pizza that summer. With the kids being home all the time, my check and Mom's was not enough.

Ingrid got in trouble several times for jury tampering. She was very much involved in her son's sick world. I believe she condoned it. We found out later he had more than two priors on family members from years ago in Texas and more recently in Springfield, Missouri. It all made me sick to my stomach! I started immediately wondering what the fuck was going on with my sister.

How could my sister end up in this situation? They had to be wrong, but they were not wrong. She left him clearly after she saw him doing something to Harley because we found out she called Harley's dad, Terry in Texas and told him she caught Peewee doing something to Harley. And Terry called 911 from Texas and had the cops do a well child check, and when they got there, Heather was bashing out Pewee's car windows with a baseball bat. They took Harley to the hospital. She suffered damage. He had used things on her and she was hurt badly. She was incontinent and they said sexual torture was the charge Peewee ended up with after it was all done. He went to jail that day for first-degree child molestation and my sister went for property damage. They were both released after twenty hours and both took off together. My sister got really mad that

I got the kids from Ingrid. She was furious! She even called DFS on me and Momma, saying we were unfit and I was selling my meds and eating patches. That had been months ago. The only thing we were doing was smoking pot, but me and Momma were contacted by DFS to do a drug test. The pot alone was enough to lose all the kids, so we both hurried up and drank vinegar and passed our test and were granted foster guardianship of Dylan, Sebrina, and Zachary. We had a lot of things to comply with for Family Services to keep being foster parents to my nephews and my niece Sebrina. We had to be able to financially provide them food and other items like a fire extinguisher, which I was glad to get. The kids also needed clothes.

DFS let us know, if we couldn't handle taking care of three extra kids, they would remove them. We were terrified of being separated. My utilities were in a friend's name and they found out and shut the power off. I had no clue how I was going to pay the $2500 passed due bills in mine and Mom's name. Plus, they wanted a combined $300 deposit so that totaled $2,800. That is what I needed right then to get power back on. We found friends to stay with that were safe until we got it figured out. That took three weeks! We were having weekly DFS meetings at the house and she had no clue the power was off. At that exact moment, the power was getting turned back on. The Guardian at Leighton showed up unannounced to see the kids and she realized what was going on. I told her all about the utilities situation and she told me she was taking the kids! Dylan went out the back and ran away to his friends and contacted me later, but Sebrina and Zachary were placed in foster homes.

Dylan contacted me and I made sure he was taken care of until Heather got out. He said he would turn himself in, he just wanted to wait until after his 16th birthday and it was not that far away from his birthday. I thought that sounded reasonable.

CHAPTER SEVENTEEN

I wasn't supposed to be talking to my sister, but I was because I needed to understand exactly what happened because the things the detective was telling me did not match up with my sisters character at all. They were insinuating that Heather was in on the sexual abuse. I did not believe that at all. But I needed to know why she went to Utah with him. The detective I spoke with that was in charge of the case told me that Heather said my nephew, her son, who was eleven, needed to be looked at for what happened to Harley. She seemed very worried about Dylan and was ready to start hanging missing person signs. I felt bad, so I told her I knew where he was and he was safe. She immediately turned him in, but she was living with a church lady of Ingrid's. I found it odd that Ingrid also paid a lot of money for my sister's car to be brought from Utah to Springfield, Mo. But we would eventually have our day in court. My nephews and niece were gone and I felt depressed about losing them. I decided I would move near Twila, who was living north of town, kind of in the country. I told my doctors my arms were still hurting from nerve damage, still really bad, and they didn't hesitate to give me my patches back. It was in no time that I would OD or just withdrawal, I think.

I had never felt this way. I know that it was so bad. I was so sick that I said I could never eat a patch again. I was off of them maybe two months. Heather, my oldest sister, showed up to take me and my kids to church, and I was too sick, so I asked her to please just take my girls. They didn't need to be around me like that and see me so sick. She refused to take them. I could not understand when I lost my sister when she became an evil monster instead of the hero I knew her to be growing up. So I took myself off the fentanyl and never touched it again till this day. I can't stand the smell of hand sanitizer because that's what it tasted like. Alcohol would become my biggest demon.

That would be what brought out my evil monster. We were living in the country and the girls had just ended 2010 summer. I had a pool set up for them since I couldn't take them swimming and they loved the country life. They were little explorers just like me, but there were a lot more adventurers like catching snakes. They loved them, had absolutely no fear of any little critters or creatures.

The snake situation got so bad I had to get a Missouri conservation book about snakes to see which ones were okay and which were poisonous. I remember that was after Keannah, age four, came running in asking me to come see the giant snake Kaleah had under the barrel. She meant the wheelbarrow. Yeah, my girls took straight to the country living. I went and saw this huge snake in. Kaleah and Keannah were sitting on top of this wheelbarrow just as happy. They were excited about the big catch. I was not as thrilled, I was mortified. I immediately got them in away from the five-foot serpent. I called Inez because Inez knew everything about country living. I asked her and she told me it was a harmless black snake and to leave it be. It would keep the poisonous ones away. I wasn't going to argue, but I also did not encourage the girls to keep playing with their new friend either. I tried my hardest to lift myself up for my girls as best I could, but the truth is, I was in pure mental and emotional hell, and physical pain sometimes. One thing I would do to show my kids love was cook for them and make it really special. I had nothing else to give them, and I hated it.

I made up games for us like Sally from the Valley where I would dress like a funny waitress. I would change my voice and go around and take their orders and make menus of a few things we had quick to make and they would laugh and play along. It was the best of times we ever had. Looking back now, that was priceless. But I got sick of not having money for my kids and living from monthly check to monthly check. Sick of my kids knowing they would never get a game station or wear the new fun shoes that were also skates. I wanted to give my kids everything like in my original plan, but I wouldn't be able to with an SSA check, that's for sure. And becoming a famous actress wasn't looking promising and taking any chance on getting my babies woke up by agents in all black was definitely not happening! So I had a plan to invest my money in a dude I was seeing. I would throw him $500 and have him double it for me.

I got a part-time job working on the phone doing what I had done years ago on the phone set appointments. But now I wasn't doing any good on the phone. It was like they could hear the anger in my voice, and people who used to always respond to me would just slam me back-to-back. I found myself saying shit other weak people used to say that I thought were not putting their all in. And worst of all, my manager was a guy I first trained when he was 16 years old, now he was my boss riding my ass. Ain't that a bitch?

At least I had my boy Kade flipping my $500 for me, because it looked like my job wasn't working out. Me and Twila went to the club to let off some steam and we were popping Xanax and drinking, and I decided to go see Kade because he had not answered my call that day. We got there and I saw Bobby's other baby momma there, and she knew that me and Kade were together. They were on the balcony telling me fuck me, they got my money and fuck me. So I freaked out and told them to let me in. They wouldn't let me in. So I got on top of her car and proceeded to use it as a trampoline. I busted every window on that car and dented the hood with my high heel knee boots I was wearing. I ended up in jail that night. I got out of jail, and now I had lost $500 we didn't have to lose and my job, so the rent didn't get paid. We got evicted, but I found us a house just in time for the sheriff to come and put our stuff on the lawn. We got moved into the new house. It was big, ugly, and scary, but it was ours!

We lived in the hood on a hot block in Springfield, right off Chestnut Expressway and Grant in a big scary house and I was trying to make the best of it. But it was hard when I kept thinking about how successful I once planned to be at twenty-five years of age. We lived close to one of the most redone parks with the most fun pools with the most up to date equipment in an effort to clean up the community, because the park was known for illegal activity. It was across from an elementary school, and it is where you start cleaning up in a neighborhood with the kids. Obviously we had constant police activity, so one way I earned respect was to watch the houses that weren't bad dudes, just selling a little, not hurting nobody. If I saw police by their house, I would call or send them a text or a code. There were three houses I kept an eye out for and they watched out for my kids and me. That's how poor neighborhoods work. But I could not have the chance of my house looking hot. As a matter of fact, I made a couple dudes pay me to pull up next to my house, because I figured you're not going to make money and make my house hot for free. That's not happening.

I was crazy and I demanded respect. Turns out his girl in the passenger seat had been stuck in Green County Jail with me and was needing $100 to get out and she didn't know any numbers. She had just moved here from St. Louis. I will never forget the COS in the jail was so rude. They made her take her braided in weave out in a humiliating way. I will never forget seeing her crying while she was doing it and she was not allowed to eat until she was done removing it. So when I got out, I boned her out and she gave me a 32-inch flat screen TV. She was cool so her boyfriend understood and showed me the respect I deserve. There was a time during this time where I did thirty days in jail. That was before I bonded out Landa. That's actually how I met her.

I had to do thirty days for noncompletion of SATOP from a DWI I got when I was 18, but I was doing thirty days when I met Felicia. She had been in the county almost three months when I got there to complete my thirty-day shock and we became friends. She was a meth addict and always talked about wanting to stay clean. I respected that. One day she got mail saying she could still fight for her kids instead of losing them to the state. I was so excited for her.

I told her she could stay with me and that I did not do meth and that I had my time to do it. But since it was only $100 for her to get out, I was sure my momma needed help with the house and kids. So when our checks came three days before I was to be released, I had my Momma bond Felicia out. I told her to go to my house, shower, shave and help Mom and just eat good. I would be home I think it was going to be a Friday at 11:33pm.

I was so excited to go home and kiss my babies. Besides when I was in the hospital, I had never been away from them. So I had my momma bond Felicia out three days before me and I got out as scheduled. I got home and woke all my babies up and I was hugging them so tight and crying because I was so happy to be back with my babies! Kayden said to me, "Momma, your friend borrowed my phone and went outside the other day and has not been back."

I asked my mom, and yes, she confirmed that Felicia came, changed and took off with some of my clothes and Kayden's phone. I kissed my kids and put them back to bed. I put my tennis shoes on and went to every dope house in the neighborhood and put word out to everyone that I wanted her found! It was the following Wednesday when my homeboy Q came through around 10:30 am and said Felicia was at the motel and I needed to get there before checkout.

We pulled into the hotel she was at. She wasn't there, but a girl named Tina told me she had moved to another hotel and said she would make sure I could get her that day. In that moment all kinds of things were going through my mind, but most all I was wondering whether this bitch was going to apologize to my daughter. So I was going to take her to my house and she would clean until she had worked off the phone, the bond and the straight disrespect. Then I would let her go. But that's not how it went. When we pulled in the motel, she was standing right outside and I jumped out and at first, I was really trying to put her in the car, but she was probably three times my size, me weighing maybe 130 pounds. But I was trying. I yelled out, "Q, help me!" Q said, "Nope, I don't want no part of a hostage situation." I just punched her until I couldn't anymore. Then I kicked till I couldn't kick anymore, then proceeded to punch her and so on until I got tired. Later on, after I got into recovery, I made amends with Felicia in 2020. It's never too late to do the right thing and own your part.

Chapter Eighteen

At this point, it was Christmas 2010 and Gerdy, my friend that I had known since I was 14, the one that helped me bust Bobby with the DNA test, had gotten into escorting prostitution. She would charge $100 an hour or $60 for half-hour for any sexual favor, oral, or full sex with condom. She told me this as she was smoking meth and I was sitting there drinking and popping Xanax. I couldn't believe what she was telling me. I was sad for her. She said she would pay me $50 to ride with her because it would be safer than her going by herself. So I started riding with her. I was watching her get maybe six to ten clients a night, and was never inside more than thirty minutes, no matter if they smoked meth, and also had sex or just oral. She was using a different name. She would go by Sharya. She was dirty and sloppy about it. After maybe three days of riding with her, I learned how to make my own website ad to get clients. But I would perfect mine and do the complete opposite of Gerdy.

I was going to be classy and keep it as professional as possible. I looked at the ads available, my competition and what the donation was for in call (which meant I had a place) and out call (which mean they did). My first rule was always go high on donation, a maximum of $2000.00 or minimum of $1500.00. If they went for it, it meant they were either cops or a killer, so I would set up the date and give wrong information. Rule 2: No truck drivers! Too nasty and scary! Rule 3: No Mexicans or black men. No one I would actually date. Rule 4: Always wait for big money. Less customers, more money was key. Rule 5: Never go to cheap hotels. Only four stars.

Rule 6: If I go to their home, take someone with me, or always let someone know who I am with and where I am going, especially my Momma. I told my Momma everything. No secrets between us. I made a minimum of 600 or 400 a half-hour and saw maybe three clients a day in the beginning. And then the site blew up and prices dropped drastically. I figured I could make a bunch of extra money and it wouldn't put my kids at all in jeopardy of the agents kicking the house in again. It was very dangerous, but so was my depression watching my kids use soup cans to get in the pool at 5:30 to swim till 6:30 and having to watch them cry because I couldn't take them to swim at the lake or river. But if I had money, I would pay someone or send them to places and get them ice cream when the ding ding (ice cream) man came through, it made me feel less than. I did teach my girls how to make sweet Southern-style cold cups. And in the summer of 2011, they started selling them and made good money. They continued to make them every summer till they all turned sixteen and got jobs. I am proud I taught them that skill and they kept up. Hopefully they will teach my future grandchildren.

It was this time I met a young girl, Whitney, who was sixteen and just quit high school. She seemed to take to me right from the beginning in the mother role. Her mom Barbara had been in prison and would not be released for a few more years, so Whitney moved in with us and would help me a lot with the girls. She till this day calls them her sisters. I would make sure they had money to go swimming and have fun at the pool, and we became family for life. Also, when her momma got out of prison, we all became close. God works like that. He brought us together to help us all.

Over the next couple years, every month or so for a few weeks at a time, I would escort and travel within 100 miles of Springfield. Heather had done everything she needed to do to get the kids back. She got a house, she just needed house supplies, and I was happy to help her get everything she needed; furniture, beds, dressers, TVs, dishes, and pretty much anything I could do to make her house be ready for them to come home. Heather was also getting stuff to make the house as cozy as possible. I got her everything they needed and yes, I paid for it with my body. I would turn on actress, the alter ego Ms. Rain. I was a glamorous woman who would fulfill your husband's or your dad's fantasy at the finest hotels. I would demand to be treated like a lady.

I was once tipped 1200.00, and another client tipped me a real Tiffany necklace. I would be contacted by local celebrities and they would be my clients. I still cringe today at some commercials when I see him on TV.

I was contacted by a man by mistake one time who just simply did not recognize me but was a part of my life when it got burned. That ended with him saying, "Hannah, your kids need this. Just take it," and handing me over 600. That person was kind. He said, "We are friends. Let's just let me get you home." I cried the whole way. When I got home, I told Momma everything and I just cried on her chest. My safe place. I loved Momma.

So I'm talking about making money from selling my body for every client I see. I took at least two showers and two bubble baths, never anything less, in between clients no matter what. Sometimes I would just stay in the jacuzzi for hours, but I did what I did the safest way I knew I did and always wore a female condom up in me and one of them for everything. Always safe. Sometimes I would use a bottle of body wash in less than 24 hours. Alcohol, Xanax and money would keep me awake, so I would bring home thousands of dollars in presents all the time and I would pay Whitney to take the girls swimming. I would give them $30 to get in and $100 for whatever they wanted. And we didn't have money issues anymore. I loved to spoil the kids as much as I could.

Every few months I would work a couple weeks escorting and we would live good, with no worries about police knocking on my door. My family life was separate. The fast money I was making was destroying my soul. I never felt so nasty. Poor inside and beautiful outside. It was disgusting! It was clear they felt powerful to purchase "The MS Rain." I specified I did not run specials. I am the special and I'm a lady first, so treat me accordingly! I started losing clients due to the increase in sex trafficking.

In fact, those poor girls were being sold for $40. I remember constantly seeing 60/40 minutes on most ads. Very few were even trying to get the $100 and I thought, *I'm going to have to change things up and do it quickly!* Gerdy gave up and just settled for $40 and was grateful for $60 clients, doing it out of her apartment where her kids were living. There was no shame in her game, but that was while she was on meth. Meth will destroy you. The cheaper clients I was getting fueled my anger for husbands that mistreated their families. The longer I was escorting the more my anger for men grew. The way they were disgustingly disrespecting their wives really got to me.

I decided to start arranging big money overnight or even over the weekend dates. Minimum of $800 up to $3,000 for all weekend. Except I would always get the money as soon as I got there, even if it was for just 30 minutes. I would make sure they had gotten me my favorite alcohol. I would make them a drink and me one. But I would put some crushed up melatonin in it. I knew it was harmless because I gave it to my kids, the strawberry dissolving kind to make them sleep when it was summer, turning back to school time and they needed to get back on schedule. But I would give these men more depending on their size. I would take pics of their ID and message it to them after I took whatever cash they had or anything of value from them, plus taking my donation. I had done that several times, and then it got way too risky when I arranged a date like that and my GPS said, "You are here." I heard gunshots. I was being shot at. I got myself safely away and far from there and checked into a room and never went back. I decided I was going to stop robbing clients.

It was about that time I would decide, while driving around Missouri alone doing escorting, that I would stop at my dad's grave to put my kids and my pictures on his headstone. I was going to make sure his black grandbabies and myself were there for everyone to see, not just "Husband of Katherine." It made me sick that I was not represented in my dad's life on his headstone. I knew how much he loved me. I was the only person he really never tried to hurt. I took pride in that. I also believed in my heart he would have loved my children. I dreamed once he was watching TV with them and looked back at me and winked with a big smile of approval. So I was going to get those pictures on there. I would tape them to his headstone the best I could, pictures of me and my girls. I put maybe ten pictures covering my stepmom's name up. I felt justified and I was also feeling extremely emotional about my life and how it was spiraling into something I couldn't recognize. I taped the pictures on his headstone in the Platt Cemetery. It made me feel glory for some reason. After that, I headed home to Momma and my girls.

I got home and decided I was done escorting and I wouldn't do it again! We were living off the bare minimum monthly check and getting better, it seemed. I did manage to move us into a nice home. It was green and beautiful and a better neighborhood. We were doing okay, even started going to Freeway Church. I felt huge convictions for what I had been doing and I ended up having a complete breakdown and I broke everything in my room. I broke my TV, three full-length mirrors, my stereo, and I was just out of my mind crying and wanted to be done living with the pain! Momma called 911 and they took me to the psychiatric unit for adults at Marion Center where I was as a teenager and had stayed three times prior. I would be in there for a while trying to get help. I got out after almost two weeks and went home to Momma and the kids and was feeling better.

That lasted a while. During this time period, my oldest sister got the kids back, Dylan, Sebrina and Zachary. Almost as soon as DFS was out of her life, she would take off on us again. My sister was very extreme. If she was using, she went hard and it was as if we didn't matter, her kids didn't matter, no one but the man in her life, for however long they stuck around. She was hard on Sebrina. I never understood it, but I had no problem always keeping all my nephews in nieces around and also making sure everyone had what they needed. So I would take a client here and there. We had to have food and my sister would sell all her food stamps. I learned I could be a dominatrix, a female master, and I would get paid so much more money than having sex with a client! Being a dominatrix meant men would pay me to humiliate and even slap and beat them. It was a lot of money. The least amount made was maybe $300 just for a client to walk into my classy hotel room and let me slap him one time. It took fifteen seconds. It was crazy how much money they would pay. I was in disbelief. One client, after three hard spankings and donating $500 said quickly, "I have to hurry home to my wife." I thought to myself, *I wonder if she knew if she knocked the hell out of her husband how much of a better marriage they would have?* I would also think, *Why didn't these guys just go somewhere and easily get themselves beat up for free?* Cause some of them wanted to be tortured and well. I was glad to torture a man! I'm your girl all day, no problem. Well, most of the time. Some things I wouldn't do. Like the guy who wanted to be castrated, he kept calling me. I put a new ad up with a new number for safety but got sick of feeling disgusted at how I was living my life.

Plus, everything had started to change. My sister got clean on her own and started taking care of her kids. She had relapsed on meth and the kids would mostly stay with me 90% of the time. It wasn't until she met her now husband that she would settle down. My nephew

Dylan at age sixteen ran away from the group foster home they put him in and didn't get out till he was seventeen. It was the summer of 2012 and we lived in the beautiful green house and my sister lived in the duplex across the street with her new husband Willie and the kids. Dylan was even home. She was trying to keep the kids away from me, the niece and nephews I had basically helped raise an at times she forced on me and Momma. Although we had never minded one bit. This was crazy to me. The only thing I cared about in this whole world was my family. I would do anything for any of them!

My sister's husband seemed OK. He was a recovering addict, off meth, although arrogant and a definite know it all that had done and seen everything. I thought he loved my sister, and why should I care if he is annoying? I was not married to him. That's her forever! If she was happy, I was happy for her.

Chapter Nineteen

We ended up having to move because of my break-down. Plus, the landlord showed up and saw me and Momma were smoking cigarettes in the house and we also had gotten a dog, so all of this violated our lease agreement. It was hard finding a landlord to rent to me and Momma with our rental background. We found a place on East Pacific Street in North Springfield and would move in on Momma's birthday, August 1, 2012. She would be fifty-seven. It would take every penny, and I mean every penny of our checks to move. We did not even have enough to buy one pack of cigarettes, much less a birthday present for Momma. We were getting moved in and I saw a beautiful woman outside washing a classic car, an old station wagon. It was me-tallic green, probably a late '70s model.

I noticed she looked like a sweet angel and she had long, golden, thick brownish hair. She had all kinds of beautiful flowers in her yard. I usually never met neighbors that we got along with, usually because they did not like my black kids or, in the early days, my partying, depending on the neighborhood. But this lady seemed different. So, at first, I just waved at her and she waved back while continuing to wash her car while we continued to move into our new home two doors down from her.

Later that day, I was wanting a cigarette really bad and so was Momma. I had reached out asking anyone that was coming to bring us some, but I was impatient. I went to knock on the lady's door I had seen and waved at earlier. I got close and could hear a familiar song I liked playing loudly! As I got to the door, I could smell the sweet smell of marijuana. Now I knew we was going to be friends for sure. I knocked and she answered sweetly in her kind voice, "Yes, can I help you, sis?" I said, "Yes, ma'am. We just moved in and no worries. Your house smells wonderful. Ours smells the same usually." I asked her if she had a cigarette. I told her it was also Momma's fifty-seventh birthday and we spent everything moving two doors down and if she had a cigarette and maybe a bowl, we would definitely pay her back in the future. She went and bought me and momma each a pack of cigarettes and she also smoked a bowl of pot with us. That was the start to how Ms. Kay became family. She would remain in our lives every day forward from then on. Ms. Kay loved the girls. She even walked Kaleah and Keannah to school the first day that year. Their school was on our street just four blocks down. Ms. Kay just fit right into our family.

Ms. Kay had a thirty-year-old daughter that was pregnant and due with a boy, but she was having him with a doula in Rogersville, Mo in a birthing tub and Ms. Kay wasn't able to be a part of her only grandchild's birth. This made her very sad! It also made her cling to us and we clinged back. We loved her from the start. I would always make enough dinner to take Ms. Kay a plate. I will never forget how much she raved about everything I cooked, especially fried chicken. But potato salad was her absolute favorite. Every time I made it, no matter what, I made sure she got some, and for years she always said the same thing: "Sis, this potato salad just gets better every time you make it." I looked forward to making plates and sending them over to her. I would send the girls to take it. She swore I was trying to fatten her up! We were family though, not just neighbors or even friends. She was my sister twister. Plus, she was just a few years younger than Momma and it gave Momma someone to confide in.

We would meet Ashli after her baby boy was born at the end of August when she brought him to meet his grandma, Ms. Kay. Ashli was such a sweet girl and looked like she could be my little sister with red hair and blue eyes. She was so beautiful and such a sweet soul and giving heart like a mother. She moved in with her momma soon after Hilton was born and we were all very happy to see them be able to share the moments of their bonding with baby Hilton's arrival. Also, Ms. Kay would now split and fight with Ashli over my potato salad because both just loved it so much and could not get enough. They were so funny!

Ashli really took to Keannah, who had just turned seven that August. Ashli would take her and her son, baby Hilton, on picnics and read them books almost every day after school. Keannah was struggling in school and Ashli jumped at the chance to tutor her. After all, Ashli was a college graduate that drank but didn't do any drugs. She barely smoked on occasion. Keannah and Ashli were best buddies. I loved the positive influence Ashli was. God knows I was definitely not the best influence on my kids after everything I put them through trying to survive life after being burned. I absolutely hated the mom I was; it was not the mom I planned or wanted to be for my babies.

It was almost Christmas 2012 and my sister and Willie had contacted me saying that they were being evicted and would be homeless. Although Willie still had his job at the rock company, they had nowhere to go with my nieces and nephews. We just happened to have a garage in the back that could be livable if worked on correctly. My sister was clean off of meth and so was he, but she was still being prescribed high doses of hydrocodone and Willie was still buying more with his weekly paychecks, sometimes upwards of $10 a pill, with her eating two at a time almost three times a day, maybe even more. It started from a back injury she said she got from working at the newspaper, but my sister was always secretive about anything she did. I'm sure you can guess that already. Anyway, I let them move into the garage and set it up how they wanted.

My sister would be in either an extreme high or manic state. There was never any telling because she was suffering with mental illness. She had been seeing a doctor for a couple years since everything with Harley. She would flip out on the kids a lot, especially Sebrina. One time I can remember she made spaghetti out in the garage and Sebrina thought she was helping and made some corn to go with it. My sister went off on her as if she was the worst child in the world, making my niece cry and hurting her feelings. I always felt so bad for Sebrina, taking the mental and physical abuse from her mom. My sister had the greatest idea to make the electric pole Apt B at my house, which was illegal by city code standards and completely ridiculous. She did paint it with pretty flowers and made it look appealing but she was out of her mind. I never charged them rent because I wanted them out as soon as possible.

My sister was spiraling out of control. Anything could set her off. It reminded me a lot of dealing with my dad, walking on eggshells constantly. This was my house, I was an adult and I didn't put up with people's shit, but I was worried about my niece and nephews. Also, you have to remember, she had just tried keeping them away from me the year prior when she married Willie, so I was grateful to have them around and their help, even after all the bad things she had done to me and to them. I was biding my time until they got their taxes and could get the fuck out.

My sister and Willie moved out with the kids and finally got a place of their own, and that seemed to be working out. At least they were out of the house. My nephew Dylan was seventeen years old and had brought a girl around a couple times. Then she all of a sudden said she was pregnant with his baby and had a baby girl who they named Kliemie, but her grandmother took her away from us and never let us see her. I still hope she finds me one day. Last time I saw Kliemie, it was spring 2019. We decided to move from Pacific Street to around the corner from Ms. Kay, so we were still really close.

Ashli had lost her son to DFS for mental health reasons in summer 2013. On August 4, 2013, Ashli went in her mom's backyard, poured gasoline on herself, and set herself on fire. She was pronounced dead when help arrived. At the exact moment she had done this, her mom, Ms. Kay, was picking up my best friend, Amanda V, to bring her to my house, and I have always felt responsible even though I know I'm not. But Ms. Kay was doing something to help me at the moment her daughter was dying. Ms. Kay found a suicide note in the book that Ashli had used to read to baby Hilton every night when she got her phone call visit. It read that she loved her mom and that her mother would be rich beyond the world's dreams, that she hoped her father had gotten what he wanted and that this was a Buddhist sacrifice.

The receipt from the gasoline purchase read 05:23 pm. Ashli called her mother at 05:27 pm and asked her where she was and sounded fine. Ms. Kay said she was helping Amanda get to my house because her boyfriend was being mean to her and she needed to get away. Ashli had acted normal and said she loved her and hung up the phone. The first 911 call was made for Ashli by me when the kids were coming in screaming about the fire. I had called at 05:36 pm, so by my personal investigations along with Ms. Kay's information, after she got off the phone with her mom, Ashli immediately killed herself. What was crazy to me and also was spoken to me by God after the fact was what the coroner's report said. Ashli set herself on fire but died of gas inhalation. I had swallowed gas, was set on fire and burned 67% and here I stand with mostly just my arms scarred. The neighbors who were outside all playing said they hardly heard one scream. This was 05:30 pm on 1 August in a neighborhood full of kids. I know when I was on fire all I could do was scream. I researched Buddhist sacrifice. It is something that is done in the daytime to protest something you strongly disagree with. You basically protest by setting yourself on fire in public.

This sent Keannah on a downward slope of depression, anxiety and PTSD. She was only seven, almost eight, but it would be a couple years before I saw the true effects. She would also find a cross that came out of nowhere that no one had given to her. She said it was from Ashli. Ms. Kay decided to have a celebration of life, not a funeral. It turned out beautiful and amazing, just like Ashli. I spoke on how she touched my life and I loved hearing how she touched other people's lives and the stories I heard from her friends she went to college with. Everyone had amazing things to say about her, but no one spoke more amazing than Ms. Kay, who was a true child of God in every way. A sister of Jesus. Kaleah and her friends sang a beautiful song in tribute to Ashli. Kaleah has the most beautiful voice. The celebration was beautiful, packed and was standing room only. Ms. Kay had her cremated and put in a silver and baby blue urn with doves on it. She brought it home and left it at the end of her bed.

I can't make this up, literally. The evening of the celebration, we came home to our house flooding from the upstairs bathroom into the downstairs light fixture. I was so freaked out because it was going into the light fixture and because of my fear of fires, I called 911. They told me to call a plumber or my landlord immediately and to shut off the water. There was no shutoff in the upstairs bathroom, so I had to shut the water off completely from the mainline outside. My landlord literally lived next door and was a junkie. I could sit at my kitchen table drinking beer and playing spades and watch the dope man serve him every hour and half. He didn't even have his phone bill paid, but I went and banged on his door when my house was flooding and told him I needed help. He told me that plumbing was my responsibility and it was on the lease I had signed before I moved in. I told him he was fucking crazy and I was calling the Health Department.

The house started molding immediately. The mold was growing at a rapid pace, starting in the hallway under the bathroom that was upstairs. It was growing as fast as I could wipe it clean with bleach, it was so bad.

All of a sudden, just a few days later, the kids were telling Momma goodnight and came up and told me she has a basketball on her stomach and that I needed to come look. Mind you, I had been in a serious depression, so I hadn't been downstairs in a while. I went down there and realized there was something wrong with my mom, so I called 911. They came and got mom and took her to the ER. I followed the ambulance. Amanda V had stayed with the kids. They had to rush my mom in for hernia surgery. It did not look good when she came out of surgery. She was on a ventilator at this time.

My sister Heather showed up out of nowhere in the ICU, screaming profanities about me being a prostitute whore. She was escorted out by security. It was a complete shock to me because we had not been fighting. The last time I'd seen Heather, we were laughing. I was completely caught off guard by how she was acting, especially while our mom was so sick. She ended up being escorted out of the hospital, by hospital security. When I needed her the most, my sister just came out of nowhere fighting with me. That's the monster she had turned into, and I didn't even recognize the hero she used to be when we were kids. That had actually been years ago and I didn't know we were fighting, but since my mom was not doing good, the hospital said we had to alternate visits because there was no POA (power of attorney) in place and she was unable to make medical decisions for herself. So the next day Mom woke up and I was so relieved. They moved her out of ICU and the first thing we did was give me POA. She ended up coming home where she had a nurse come in every day. By then we had to turn the water on a few times to cook and clean, and every time we turned it on, the water in the house got worse and worse, leaking through the ceiling and the mold was just accumulating.

I wiped it all down with bleach one day. Let me add that me and my mom both have COPD. The day after I wiped it down, it came right back. The nurse that was coming in every day was a mandated reporter and hot-lined adult services on me, but I was happy because when I called the Health Department, they told me everything was fine and there was nothing they could do by her reporting me to the hotline. It actually helped. It was funny how they didn't really care about my kids living in that situation, but because Mom had a gaping wound that had to be clean twice a day, it was a risk of infection and safety for her. They ended up helping with resources and we got moved into a different house. We were really worried about having to move away from Ms. Kay, but it still ended up being within walking distance. All was well.

We were moved. Mom was healed up.

Sebrina actually graduated high school in 2015 and was pregnant with a baby boy on the way. I couldn't have been happier. Rather than escorting or being a dominatrix, I decided to find me a sugar daddy. That's where the money was going to come from. I had no desire to have a boyfriend since all the previous ones had been abusive or liars or junkies and had shown me that within a week of meeting them. I started my search on different websites. I was interested in the ones you had to pay for. I started reading reviews and doing research. I found a site and filled out the info and took some cute pics, none of the ones from my old ads. I needed to be up to date, fresh, and what they were looking for. Unique and exotic. I'm a redhead, so I had that already going for me. I got a few bites. I can tell you with certainty it was a Thursday night I met this guy named Barry. He was from Kansas City. We both seemed like we were looking for the same thing. He wanted to spoil and I wanted to be spoiled. He also told me he was impotent and liked doing oral, which I was fine with.

He was in his late fifties and had been single for more than twenty years. He had a huge savings for the right girl to spend. Barry said he would come down tomorrow to meet me, which was going to be Friday. I asked how long he could stay and would he take me to Branson to go shopping. He replied that he had to be back in KC by Monday. I asked him to hold on while I checked resorts and hotels in Branson. I quickly found one of the finest hotels with a jacuzzi suite and sent him the confirmation number along with the price and asked him if that would work. It was a large price. I could not remember how much, but I was testing the waters to see how much he was willing to spend. I also added that I would need new clothes for sure and toys for my kids while I was on my trip.

He said no problem. He came down the next day and before we left Springfield I had him spend $500 at the adult store on sexy outfits to keep him happy all weekend. We got to Branson and I spent a few thousand at the outlets. We went to the hotel. He hadn't batted an eye about any of the money I had already spent. He was willing and was a nice guy. He had actually gotten some medicine that was supposed to help with his erectile dysfunction, but it seemed to be making him sick and I was concerned. I told him it was definitely not a problem. We had a great weekend. Basically, by Sunday night I had Barry willing to do anything for me. He was even going to stay another night to buy me an SUV before returning to KC. Winter was coming and he didn't want my kids walking to school, and he would give me the title and sign it over to me. Everything was unbelievable. He was even good looking for an older guy. I thought he had a very high-ranking job where he worked and had a large life savings.

I got me an almost brand-new Ford Expedition, fully loaded, paid for in cash with tags and full coverage insurance. He gave me a credit card and headed back to Kansas City. I immediately went home, picked up my mom and the kids, and we went shopping. I also learned a lot about online shopping. Then they shut the credit card off a couple of times. It was his actual bank card, so he would have to call and have them turn it back on. It was just annoying, but whatever. I was spending his money left and right and he never complained. Eventually the title got mailed to his house and I drove up there to get it. That was around Valentine's Day. We had a fun weekend and also went to his bank where he put me on his bank account with my ID included. I got my title that he signed over to me for less than 100 so I could get it all in my name. I went home. Everything was going good for a couple more weeks. Then, just before my thirty-fourth birthday, Barry told me that he was going to be buying a house in KC and that his savings was almost gone. He asked how much I made in SSA because we needed to discuss a budget. That wasn't what our relationship was based on.

I distinctly remember meeting him on a sugar daddy type of website, not a Christian or match type website. The arrangement was made and it was a financial one and did not include my finances or me leaving Springfield, where all of my family was. Not to mention my mother, who had countless health problems already and multiple doctors' appointments every month. Needless to say, me and Barry's relationship ended at this time. I pray that he found someone.

Chapter Twenty

It was the beginning of the summer of 2015. Sebrina was pregnant and living with me. I was thirty-four, Dylan was twenty-one, Sebrina was seventeen, Zachary was sixteen, Kayden thirteen, Kliemie twelve, and Keannah was nine years old. I was set to move into a brand-new house, finally getting out of all the nasty houses I had gotten, my rental history set and in good standing. I was also dating an old friend named Freddy. He had always seemed silly and chill and just smoked pot. I knew he hustled on the side, but that didn't bother me as long as he kept it away from my kids, and our home. The day we were supposed to move, my check didn't come. I instantly felt like this was karma from how I did Barry, and I would feel this karma for a long time. We were instantly homeless.

I was also hearing through the grapevine that my nephews were doing meth and that Dylan had done meth with his mom and Willie back when Kliemie was born. That would explain her outburst more. So I heard my nephew Zachary was at an apartment doing meth and I literally went over there, banged on the door, and I guess him and his friends who knew me escaped through the balcony. The lady on oxygen, who was well over sixty years old, had a meth pipe in her hand while there were little babies sitting on the couch. It took all I had not to beat the hell out of her. She was actually swinging on me, but I was dodging her attempts to hit me by slightly moving back. It was pathetic looking back on it. I should have called 911 and reported her and saved those babies that day. Jesus helped them; I pray. It's funny that Dylan was the one who snitched on Zachary that day. They were both on meth into their twenties.

So now I was homeless with my mom, my kids, and Freddy. At this point my sister and Willie did let my mom come stay with him and I ended up going to St. Louis with Freddy, where I would find out he was shooting meth behind my back. When I confronted him in front of his mom, he hit me so hard it busted my eardrum, but at the time I did not know it. I went to the hospital four days later because I could not hear out of my left ear and it was leaking bloody clear fluid. My left eye was also black and hurt very badly.

His mom was very nice to me and did not condone what he had done. Right after Freddy did that, he went back to Springfield and left me and the girls at my mom's. I was in the ICU when I had finally gone to the hospital. I was leaking spinal cord fluid. I was so scared and I lied and told them that someone had hit me with a blunt object while I was walking to the store and I said I did not know who did it. At the time I knew I had at least four dog at large tickets and one charge from stealing food. I had warrants out of Springfield and nowhere to take my kids. So I lied because we had nowhere to go. After all, I had been set on fire. A busted eardrum wasn't going to take me out. I could handle this if it meant my kids had food and a warm place to stay, and his mom was their granny. She treated them like her blood and so did his sister Tameka, that was my girls T-T and she still is to this day. They loved her food, the cabbage and catfish out the Mississippi River that she would catch and serve fresh. The kids loved the St. Louis style of living. I healed up and got out of the hospital. I had actually started boosting or stealing since my check stopped coming.

I definitely drank a lot more because of my depression as well as slept a lot because I did not want to be with Freddy. How dare he put his hands on me. Here I am in the ICU again because of a man that was supposed to love me.

This day in particular was a normal day until I heard something was going on in the girl's room between Freddy and Kayden. I heard Kayden screaming. When I got back there Freddie was hitting Kayden and I yelled for him to stop and Kayden started screaming at Freddie. I could not hear exactly what was being said, but I just know she was yelling at him, and then I heard him start to spank her. Then it got louder and louder. I ran in there and stopped it. Kayden was screaming at

Freddy, "You're not going to put your fucking hands on me!" She looked at me and said, "You may let him put his hands on you, but he's not going to put his fucking hands on me!" At this point she was crying uncontrollably. I was asking, "What in the fuck just happened?" And I was looking at Kayden all over her body, but she shied away and curled up into hiding.

I was completely upset and everything was not okay. I was telling Freddy he should have never hit my daughter. Granny came in and told me I should not undermine him in front of the kids. I tried to hold Kayden and console her but she would not let me. So I went into my room and laid down. My mind was racing. What was I going to do? We could not stay there. This was too much. The next day when Kayden came home, she had large bruises and welts all over her legs. My stomach dropped when she came in from school with her volleyball uniform on. I saw her and I didn't realize how bad it was. I started making phone calls to get money. I didn't want to call my mom and worry her because there wasn't anything she could do. But I called her anyway and told her everything. It was a few hours later that she would call me and tell me that my nephew Dylan and his friend would drive up to get me and the girls that same night.

I was so thankful he was able to come and get us. He really was a man now, although we didn't have anywhere to go. We went to Sebrina's apartment where my mom was also living. When I got there, I also noticed that she really didn't have anything for her baby boy that was on his way. So I went and stole at least ten times, each time walking out with a cart full of stuff.

I got more than enough for what my niece needed for him and then some. Sebrina moved out of her apartment and me and the girls were homeless in this abandoned apartment with Amanda V and her two-year-old baby. I was thinking about robbing a bank on Kearney Street here in Springfield when all of a sudden, I found this box and something made me look in it. I ended up finding a book of checks. I immediately ordered pizza so we could eat.

Then I thought to myself, *I bet tomorrow I could go write enough checks for under 500 and get us a room for at least a month so we could have somewhere to stay. And I will get a job at McDonald's if I have to so we can stay there. Me, Amanda, and the girls because my mom is okay with Sebrina.* At least she wasn't staying with Heather anymore. I woke up the next morning and went to the bank and talked Amanda into going with me to cash the checks—that's double the money—and we could get hotel rooms.

We got arrested at the bank and didn't even get the money. Now we were sitting in jail and I was literally having a breakdown. I told them to shoot me and that they better be glad that I just wrote the checks, because I was going to rob the bank and if I didn't get away with that, then I was going to make them shoot me. I was probably better off dead anyway, and my kids would be better off without me. I felt like I should have died in the fire so someone else could raise my kids better than I could. I was done. I had no more fight left in me, and I was serious. They put me on the Psych unit on every five minutes watch, meaning they check on me every five minutes looking through the window. It was torture being in there, and I did want to die. I would sing songs to myself like "Keep Your Head Up," and I would cry. God, I would cry. They wouldn't even give me a book because they said I could kill myself with 1000 papercuts. But yet they sent me in my cell every day with a giant bottle of cleanser and giant screws that were coming up from the ground.

I had five dog at large tickets that were misdemeanors, Class C felony stealing that were out of St. Louis, four stealing over a felony amount. Some had to do with getting clothes for my kids for school, and some were to pay our way. Life was not free and I wasn't selling my body anymore, and Freddy was a junkie, so I was doing what I thought I had to do. I had no one to help me and no one to go to. I thought I had hit my rock bottom, but it would just get worse. Yes, worse than going to jail. I also had three Class C felony forgery charges, one from trying to cash the check and two that were in my purse that I had already written on because I had planned to cash those later to get the room paid up for a whole month so we could get on our feet.

CHAPTER TWENTY-ONE

After being in medical segregation for eleven days, I moved into the population just as they moved me. My bondsman called me to tell me that Freddy was coming to bond me out that evening with $1,000, so I didn't even bother making my bunk or getting settled in. I gave all of my indigent stuff, which is what they give everyone who doesn't have money on their books, for example, hygiene products postcards to write to your family, free legal documents to correspond with facilities and lawyers. It was free weekly to offenders with no income. I wouldn't need it because I was supposed to be getting out right? It was about 10:30 pm that night when I gave up and started making my bunk.

We were in pods of women. There were three pods and each pod housed about twenty-five women. You're talking about seventy-five women having a slumber party from hell that are sleeping on bunk beds made of metal with half of an inch of mattress that I don't know what kind of material it was made of. Duct tape, vinyl. So earlier the girl across from me, who seemed to be about my age, maybe a little younger, was in jail for her first time and had been there a little while. She was very shy and timid but sweet.

She told me she was in there for writing checks at the grocery store to feed her kids. I completely related to her struggle. I don't think she even realized though, because when 10:30 came around and I realized I wasn't getting out, she started crying really hard for no reason because I wasn't getting out of jail. I started to think she was a little weird. And then she said to me while she's crying and panting, breathing heavily that she had sleep apnea and she snored really loud at night and it bothered the other girls. She said they got super upset and would come down and kick her bunk and pull her hair. I looked her straight in her face and told her, "Sis, I don't sleep at night. I would rather sleep during the day when commotions are going on and I wish a bitch would. I will catch extra charges in here." And I meant what I said.

The hardest part was not knowing when I was going to get out. Every day I was getting news about getting out, but I knew the only person I could count on was my mom, and it would take her too months of saving checks to get me out. It was almost Thanksgiving 2015 and I didn't even like calling home because it was super depressing. It was almost Kaleah's birthday, November 22. Sebrina was due with Liem any day now and calling just made me miss them so much more.

I was just waiting to hear the words, "Kendrick, go pack your shit." But I would wait longer. I would do my best to stay in there and keep my head up. I remember one night when I was keeping watch as I always did, because I could never sleep with silence. Even now I still have to have something playing while I sleep. Tonight, I would definitely have something to listen to. The girls down at the end of the pod had smuggled in some meth. I can only guess because none of them would shut the fuck up. They were as high as the Federal government and very obvious about it, singing and laughing, not their normal jailhouse fun. They were geeked up and it showed, and the girl Gracie across from me had started to snore very loud. I heard the girl that was always mean to Gracie. We will call her Gretchen. I heard her yell, "Someone kick that bitch's bed and tell her to stop snoring." I laid there calm, didn't move, didn't peep, didn't act like I was awake. Suddenly it felt like I was hunting for a stupid bitch.

She yelled out a few more times. By this time it was almost Med Pass, which happened at 04:30 am, 30 minutes before breakfast chow. I heard the swish of someone's legs coming full force towards Gracie's bunk, which was straight across from mine. I immediately jumped up and said, "Bitch, get the fuck back to your house right the fuck now. Leave her the fuck alone." She acted like she was making a beeline to the bathroom, towards the CO, and was yelling for her. The CO came and said, "Kendrick, stay on your bunk. You're not a CO." I said, "Yes ma'am, but she was fixing to kick that girl's bunk or pull her hair and I wasn't just going to sit there and let it happen." Gretchen replied, "No, I was going to the bathroom. Have master control. Roll back the camera if you didn't believe me." I proceeded to get up for Med Pass.

CHAPTER TWENTY-TWO

I remember calling home and finding out that Liem had been born. I have never in my life cried happy and sad tears at the same time. I couldn't believe I missed Sebrina giving birth. It wasn't all I missed. Kaleah's birthday also passed, and I wasn't there. That was really hard times when I didn't know when I was going to get out, but I knew I would, at least for sure get out. December 3 Mom would finally have enough to get me out with that check and her November check.

No more false hopes of getting out. Except December 3 came, and my bondsman called me upstairs and said St. Louis was going to be putting a hold on me so I would be getting transferred to St. Louis instead of getting out, and I would have to sit until close to Christmas before even getting transferred. Talk about disappointment. So I went back to my bunk and said, "It is what it is."

I give it to God. They couldn't hold me forever. On December 4, the CO yelled loud, "Kendrick, pack your shit, you're going home." All the girls that weren't haters were happy for me. Even the CO was choking back tears and told me to get out of there, but not before letting the girls get up when it was supposed to be locked down to give me a hug and say bye. This never happened for any other inmates that got out, but I guess I made my impression. I got out of jail that day and I have not returned.

So I went through all my court dates in St. Louis and Springfield and I ended up on probation for 5 years, court cost, restitution, community service and I actually ended up with three probation officers. I had Officer Sidwell for 2 years, a misdemeanor supervised parole officer for a year, and my state supervised probation officer for 5 years.

January 2016, I appeared in court on a felony case. I was sitting there waiting when an official looking lady with a clipboard walked in, and in a very stern voice told the bailiff she was looking for HANNAH KENDRICK. I thought, "This can't be good at all." I stood up and introduced myself and asked who she was. She was my traffic probation officer, Officer Sidwell. She was assigned to me regarding my prior traffic violations. She then stated that I hadn't reported in since November! I explained that I was under the impression my probation was to be unsupervised, and she replied, "Yes, I bet! Be in my office at 10am tomorrow!" I was terrified. This lady wasn't messing around, and I had clearly been misinformed or confused about the terms of my probation.

The next day I reported to Officer Sidwell for the first time. She was interesting, a very no-nonsense lady. I remember my intake with her. She asked me questions, like why was my memory so bad, why did someone my age have such bad anxiety, and why did I have COPD so young? I answered her questions honestly, told her all about the fire and my childhood. Nothing about my current issues. I didn't need her knowing all my ugly truths. She showed me compassion and empathy. She showed me she was doing her job for a reason and it wasn't her goal to lock me back up, but to make sure I obeyed the judge's orders.

That spring my COPD was so out of control I was hospitalized for it a couple times, and she let me work in her office during my community service hours. I really for the first time in my life saw compassion out of a government officer.

My state probation officer (for the felony theft charge in St. Louis) was Officer Knowles. He was not overwhelming or aggressive, he didn't have anything to prove. I could tell he held his position well. The first day I was in his office, looking around at his pictures and memorabilia, I saw a photo of a man in a suit, engulfed in flames. I went into a complete anxiety attack. I was crying, couldn't breathe, and started puking. After handing me tissues, Officer Knowles asked me if it was okay to explain the picture. I told him it didn't matter what he said, it's about what I see and what I feel, and I can't control it. He was extremely sensitive and told me I would never have to see that picture in his office again. I never did.

After 90 days my case was reassigned to Officer Grady. She would be my long-term probation officer and make an impact like no other. We had been living in the shelter over a year and I was so happy to find out we were finally getting into a house. We were so ready to leave the shelter and the life that came with it. Me drinking vodka on the curb of Commercial Street was killing my soul!

So they got us placed and we moved into a really creepy, big house on Cozy Street in Springfield. It was all ours and we had plenty of room. Before I knew it, most of the family was living with us. All my nieces and nephews were grown up and had issues and babies of their own. Sebrina had Liem, who was almost two years old, and was pregnant with Xander. Dylan had a drug problem, a very toxic girlfriend, and a daughter whom he never got to see. My nephew Zachary was in the same situation with the drugs.

My best friend Amanda was living with us. She had lost her two kids to their grandmother and was in an active battle with intravenous drug use. Amanda's boyfriend, who was a well-known white racist gang member on house arrest, lived with us, as well as her little brother Brandon. I was drinking every day, spending all my time on the couch. It was a brand-new couch and I spent so much time on it that it broke. Everyone else was high on meth and I was drunk. My kids were teenagers and did as they pleased, and actually made good decisions. I was lost somewhere in hell, inside.

I didn't shower. Didn't have one bit of energy to do or change anything. I wasn't smoking weed—I couldn't, because I was on probation. I felt miserable and it was getting worse and worse day by day.

January 1, 2018, Papa Joe proposed to Momma, and she said yes! They got married April 7, 2018. It was so amazing to see my momma marry the man of her dreams. Papa treated Momma like a queen, as she deserved to be treated her whole life. It was a very happy day for our family.

I decided to move again, but I only intended to take the girls. Everyone else needed to figure it out. Sebrina had already moved out and was going to college, while pregnant with Xander. Brandon got a girlfriend and moved to the country, got clean and started working. In May 2018, the girls and I moved into the cutest house on East Ave in North Springfield. I felt better almost immediately after moving in. I would not let anyone toxic into my space at that point. I was all about my family life, fried chicken and evenings on the porch. Ms. Kay would come over and we had good times together. I drank, but much less than before, though I started to smoke marijuana again. I went to see Officer Grady in June, who surprised me with a urinalysis. I admitted I would test positive for both alcohol and marijuana but promised that it wouldn't happen again. She sent me to get a drug assessment done. I was told to do outpatient classes at a well-known local rehab. Of course, I thought this was bullshit. They had the wrong girl! I figured I would graduate early and get this past me and move on.

My first day in class, a lady came in who I immediately felt at ease with and started talking about "mental illness recovery". In that exact moment, my life changed. She had my full attention! I wanted to know everything she knew and I wanted to do what she did for a living. I wanted to help and give hope! Her name was Ann Lewis and she was as smooth as silk. When she spoke, her words were chosen wisely. From Ms. Ann I felt love, healing, empathy, wisdom, and most of all I felt life come into me like never before. I was exactly where I needed to be, for what felt like the first time in my life. I felt amongst heroes, fighting for each of our lives and our children's lives. I was at home in my program, with my fellow sisters in recovery. From that day forward I would never be the same.

I stayed clean from alcohol for 10 months, and it was Ms. Ann who came to my house the first time I fell off the wagon and held me while I cried. She came the next day after I sobered up and took me for lunch and simply showed me love.

While in treatment I had the most amazing team, and Ms. Virginia was my counselor. She had a lot of experience in her field. She had heard every line of bullshit the English language had to offer and could spot a lie faster than a junkie could get high. She was somewhere in her seventies when we met and had been with the program since the 1980s. Ms. Virginia only wanted me to have emotional freedom and real happiness, and for God's sake to save myself and my soul. Everything else would follow. She kept a close eye on us girls, and her nuggets of knowledge I will hold forever and share with all I meet in life.

I had only been in treatment for a few weeks—just long enough to be hooked—when Brandon left his girlfriend. It was June 26, 2018 when he relapsed on meth and we almost lost him. He was in ICU for two weeks. Me and his girlfriend never left his side. Amanda was so high on meth the whole time she couldn't function. I literally lived at the hospital until Brandon was in the clear. He had three strokes and all his organs shut down. All we could do was pray. Even Ms. Ann came to the hospital and prayed over him. Amanda was a mess. She would not stop getting high. It was horrible. I was trying to stay clean from alcohol and it was everywhere, in every store. The 4th of July came and went with Brandon still on life support. Eventually Brandon pulled through. God had answered our prayers! Amanda was living with the person I suspected of giving Brandon the dope he overdosed on, and I wasn't happy about it at all. Amanda didn't seem to be living in reality. I continued in my treatment and was progressing well.

Brandon eventually came to live with me and the girls, because it was a much better environment for him. Kayden moved out sometime that summer because we were struggling to get along. Kayden, for good reason, had a lot of anger towards me for all my past mistakes.

She did not respect me so she ended up moving in with Momma and Papa. They had a two-bedroom apartment and it worked out better. I got her a car. She was working in telemarketing at a place I had once worked and making good money.

I was attending a 12-step program and had a sponsor. I was all in, giving it my everything. I even signed up for softball and played the whole season. That was a huge accomplishment for me. I will never forget how alone I felt on that team though. I remember how I just wanted to quit really bad. I felt like an outcast, and they didn't want me there. Only a couple of girls really spoke to me. I played that whole season, but never played again. I tried over the years to be friendly with the girls from my softball team, I even had one as my sponsor at one point later down my recovery journey. I realized that the program works. However, people tend to let you down and that's just life sometimes. I also knew I was done giving up and I was ready to fight hard, so if that meant crying in the outfield because no one said hello or crying my eyes out during our last game because no one wanted to take a picture with me, then so be it. I just pushed through and kept my head up. When I would see these ladies at events or meetings I would smile and act as if I was just fine and unbothered by their lack of communication. It really says something when you feel alone in a crowded room.

The one rule I did not listen to was the twelve-month rule: NO romantic relationships until you've been clean for at least a full twelve months and worked your steps. I started seeing someone. It immediately got serious. My relationship with Carlyle seemed to be what I was looking for. It felt like love at first sight. I made the decision of allowing the state rental assistance to end, because he was a hardworking man and he always said he worked to pay bills for his family and we were his family. He took pride in being a provider and wanting to help raise my kids as his, even though he came during their teenage years. He was 100 percent into us. So he was paying the rent.

He had a really well-paying job and made our family his top priority. He even spent an ungodly amount of money for Kaleah's eighth grade graduation. Unfortunately, he was repeatedly unfaithful. The first time I found out he cheated I used it as an excuse to relapse. I had stayed clean from alcohol for 10 months. It was Ms. Ann who came to my house when I relapsed and held me while I cried. She came the next day after I sobered up and took me for lunch and simply showed me love.

After finding out Carlyle was definitely not my faithful prince charming, we were never the same. The trust was broken. Not the love though, and we tried. We spent a month or so together, but it wasn't good. Neither of us were happy. Also both of us were lying. I wasn't drinking every day, but if I had an opportunity to drink without anyone knowing, I took it. He was still cheating while at work. I know, because I would check his phone.

I still managed to graduate treatment in July 2019, and after that I started drinking whenever I wanted. It was going okay, or at least it wasn't causing any life-shattering problems.

I caught Carlyle cheating again in November, and this time I made him move out. He moved to a house only five blocks down and would come over to bring food, money, cigarettes, alcohol, whatever I asked him to bring. I did his laundry in exchange. This went on for several months, until my final rock bottom during the Christmas holidays. I was extremely depressed, with a head full of information from recovery and a body full of alcohol. We did not celebrate Christmas that year because I was depressed and felt even more broken and suicidal. I wanted to ignore Christmas because I was so sad over where I was again. I was drinking every day again. I felt like I destroyed the version of me that I had worked so hard to save. I was once again up alone listening to sad and angry music and I was once again just so done with life's pain. I decided I had given up for Christmas.

I was, however, going to throw a bad ass big New Year's Eve party. I had a hook-up on free alcohol, I had probably ten bottles of hard liquor. On New Year's Eve around 7:30 in the morning, in my broken, drunken state, I had been drinking at least 3 days straight with no sleep. Poor Brandon was so concerned, he kept checking on me and I knew I was off the deep end. I needed to get help and I dialed 911. I woke Kaleah up and told her my plan to get help. She told me no, that she wasn't going to let me mess everything up and pointed out that DFS would get involved. I called for 911 to send me help, but no one ever came. I think that actually scared me the most. The next thing I knew, Ms. Kay showed up and I just could not stop crying. I just laid in my bed. Amanda showed up. I drank until around 5:30 pm that New Year's Eve 2019, but I have not had a drink since.

I attended a meeting a few days later and picked up a white key tag, which is a symbolic gesture meaning I was starting over fresh in the program. I went home and called Sandy and asked her if she would be my sponsor. She said yes! I was so excited because I truly respected and admired Sandy and how honest she was. I was excited to start recovery and work the steps, even attend the group mini holidays. A big recovery convention was coming up and I was all set to go. Carlyle was trying to get back with me, but I was pretty focused and he wasn't prepared to stop cheating. I went to the convention, which was at a four-star resort, and I had an amazing spiritual awakening. It was the best experience.

I heard speakers testify who had lived lives of such pain and loss, but what stuck out most was a man who spoke about almost killing his family while intoxicated. At that moment I heard God say that my family can help other families. The man went on to speak of his 30-plus years in recovery and his testimony resonated with me in a huge way. I needed to truly forgive my ex-husband

and really work at that if I was going to truly be at peace from the evil he had done. I had never kept Antonio from calling and being whatever kind of dad he could be from prison. I felt like my kids deserved to always be able to speak to him and ask him whatever questions they might have. Kaleah was about 7 years old and was talking to her dad and I heard her say "WHY DID YOU SET MOMMY ON FIRE?" and I heard her again say "NO! WHY DID YOU SET MOMMY ON FIRE?" Antonio told her he was sick and he was wrong and God was helping him. He was getting help from God, and he loved her and Mommy and he was so sorry he hurt Mommy and her and her sisters. I heard him crying and at that point I was still very angry. I took the phone from Kaleah and told him he was fucking an evil piece of shit, and to go into his cell and look in his bubble mirror and for him to face the weak sorry excuse for a fucking human being he was. Then I told him I fucking hated him, and I hung up.

I wanted the kids to be able to express themselves and be honest with the feelings they had. I felt this way because I understood how I felt about my dad. Even though I hated what my dad did to my family and stepmom, I had unconditional love for my dad. I felt my kids needed to have the right to choose how they dealt with their dad. I don't regret it one bit. My kids have told him how they feel and it was their choice to be angry or forgive or even ignore him. Looking back, it was a good decision I feel.

Antonio made himself available nonstop to answer any questions and try to make the best out of an extremely evil situation. He could have been a coward and not listened to the pain from me. I don't know if I would be strong enough to get cussed out like a dog over and over. I took satisfaction in being as cruel as I could be to him. I mean my tongue is my biggest weapon, and I am known for using it for evil I admit. But I felt justified completely to make Tonio feel pain. He could have been a coward and stopped trying to gain forgiveness after being cursed out and hung up on countless times, but he has never given up. I don't regret the therapeutic value in explaining to him how our kids are affected daily or how mine is because of his actions. I believe he needed to know the damage he did and feel the pain and punishment of destroying the lives God gave him to protect. I believe when he gets out of prison, his life mission should be to share his story and hopefully change some lives and turn something extremely evil into a positive by helping men and women at risk of falling into the devil's plan. I was truly able to forgive Antonio after I sent him all the crime scene photos in September of 2020. His response, after seeing all of them and what he did to my whole body, was exactly what I needed to completely let go of my anger and it let me truly heal in my soul.

At the recovery convention I made it a point to keep my phone off almost the whole weekend so I could take in everything and not get distracted. Communing with hundreds, maybe even thousands, of people in recovery is a true gift and a very special thing to be part of. I have gone every year since I started my recovery. I was to meet up with Sandy to go over my Step 1 in my guidebook, so I turned my phone on to call her and find out where we were meeting within the huge resort. A notification popped up, and it was a comment someone left on a crime scene photo of me from when I got burned. I had posted it ten weeks prior, but this comment was new. I checked it, and it was from a complete stranger who said she could see an angel's handprint on my freshly burnt face. I read that and started crying. But it was not normal tears. It was "footprints in the sand tears," the kind you cry when you see God moving in your life. The kind that only comes from your soul healing and the ability to give you peace.

I saw God's hand on my face! I had tangible proof that I'm a miracle! I'm favored, and He was there! I'm REALLY meant to be here! I had never been so high on happiness. I shared it the rest of the weekend with everyone. It was the best feeling ever! I came back so strong and felt ready for whatever. Bring it on, I was ready for recovery. I could face anything with Sandy as my sponsor and my sisters in recovery. We were a Bad Bitch Crew! I finally just laid down the law with Carlyle. I was very clear on what I wanted, and if he didn't like it, he could kick rocks. I told him that he didn't have to go to meetings with me, but I needed him to be more of a part of my recovery. He said he would be there for me, and we talked about him moving back in. He was still paying the bills, even though I destroyed his Jeep with a bat and slashed all four tires back in November when I was drinking. He forgave me and we were gonna try to make it work. I needed proof I could trust him, so one night when he stayed over, I put a free text/message recovery app on his phone. I found out he was definitely still talking to other girls. So I told him, "I accept that you have an addiction to women and I am powerless. Get the fuck out of my face." He left for two days. When he came back, he told me he had a problem with meth. He needed a sponsor and to start attending meetings. I immediately called my sponsor and hooked him up with her husband. I trusted their guidance and was so glad to have this couple help us, regardless of how we got there. I had huge respect for Sandy and Michael and the family values they shared in their marriage, so it made me feel safe. I just knew this was going to help me and Carlyle be the best we could be as a couple. Carlyle jumped right into recovery. He worked the steps and called his sponsor for everything. Then Covid hit. Meetings stopped happening and Carlyle's job wasn't going well. I really needed my meetings, so everything going on in the world was hitting me hard and making me depressed.

It was time for me to work on Step 2 of my recovery program, which is Acceptance. I answered all the questions on the worksheet in my 12-step guide and went over it with Sandy, which helped me process some of what I was feeling.

I had purchased a Jeep for Kaleah with her money and a decent amount that I put into it too, but it was a lemon. Carlyle offered to get her a new car, on the condition that she made the payments. Kaleah had a job for almost 6 months at that point and was being very responsible. We found her a car, and everything was arranged; he even had me put full coverage insurance on it. Since he was working six days a week with only Sundays off, it was really difficult to arrange a meeting to get the car. Weeks and then months passed by, and still no car—but I was paying for the insurance anyway. Finally, on Friday June 5, 2020, I told Carlyle, "I just paid the insurance again on Kaleah's car. We have to get it this weekend, it's been way too long." He didn't really respond, so I called the car guy myself to make arrangements to pick up the car. But he said that Carlyle told him to sell it the week before. I asked Carlyle why he did that and he absolutely flipped out. He started breaking the furniture in my bedroom, starting with my huge 15-inch Bluetooth speaker. He hated that speaker. He threw it on the ground, picked it up, then threw it on the ground again, over and over. Then he attacked my dresser. It was such destructive violence, something I had never seen from him before. He destroyed my bedroom, called his sponsor and left. I went to the hospital and was admitted with stroke symptoms. I also called my sponsor.

My momma was diagnosed with respiratory failure in the middle of the Covid pandemic and I didn't know if she was going to pull through, so I was completely on edge. I had so much on my mind; I'm a news fanatic, and our country was in shambles after George Floyd was murdered. I could not handle watching these things. I felt as if, between the pandemic and my momma and my relationship, everything was a loss. But then I thought, no. I was still clean from alcohol and Momma was still alive. Screw Carlyle, because I had Sandy, so my support system was solid! Well, less than a month later, at 11:58 pm, just two minutes before not only midnight, but also my six-month clean date, Sandy sent out a group text. In it, she stated that I was "not willing to do what it takes to stay clean" and she couldn't be my sponsor anymore. I was absolutely crushed; it was like being gut punched right in my chest. To this day, I still don't know why she did it. To my credit, instead of drinking—which I massively wanted to do at that point—I actually chose to attend more meetings and get a new sponsor.

That relationship didn't work out either. She couldn't find time for us to get to know each other the whole month of August, which did not work for me. She was also one of the softball ladies I played with and who had always been very cold to me. I'm not sure why I even wanted her to sponsor me.

I still needed a sponsor, so I asked myself, who do I go to for advice and encouragement? Who do I respect and trust, because this is not an easy task? I met a sweet girl in treatment named Leonna, who had been clean for a long time and was a lot farther into her steps than me. I called her a lot, and she would always put me in my place when I was wrong. So I asked her if she would be willing to be my sponsor, and she agreed. She became my sponsor and still is to this day. Leonna lets me be me in my recovery, she does not force anything. She is pure love and support for everything, but most importantly she never gives up on me. I'm better because she stands with me.

In August 2020 we lost our house, because I was used to Carlyle paying the rent and I was stuck in financial debt. Kaleah, Keannah and I went back and forth from Kayden's house to a friend's house until October, when we found a decent home in north Springfield. We still reside there today. I just turned 40 on March 11, 2021, and finally feel solid in my sobriety and in who I am as a person.

After a year clean from alcohol and two trips to the conventions, I'm now able to share my story. I take my life one day at a time from then on out and focus on me and my kids. Finding happiness in life. As for the rest of my family, Alex went on to have a family in Kansas City, MO, where he works and resides. Sebrina is college educated with two boys and a little girl on the way. I am very proud of the mother she is; she continues to further her education in the medical field. Me and my sister Roci have gotten closer and closer over the last couple years. It started with coffee talks on Saturdays, and now we talk daily. Sometimes a few times a day.

She plans to write a book and include her biography and what she endured. I'm also excited to announce we are planning a sisters' only trip for me and her this summer to celebrate 40 and fabulous. In 2021 it's us against the world.

My oldest sister Heather and her husband Willie have been in their active addiction for the past few years and refused to contact me or Momma at all. I prayed every day that my sister Heather would get better, and that God would bring her to reality and that she would get into recovery for her issues she faces mentally and with substance abuse. I had not seen or spoken to my oldest sister since March 11, 2018, which was my birthday. We did not fight at all that day and I still had no idea why she wouldn't talk to me or even our mom. I reached out to her several times. I forgave her mistakes. I found out Willie had basically put Heather out in August 2021 and she was living with Sebrina. She was highly medically mentally unstable and had an extreme breakdown and went into the psychiatric hospital, where she had a lengthy stay and was finally properly medicated. Although she still did not want anything to do with me or Momma, I was glad to hear she was doing better. My niece and nephews would update me.

On November 3, 2021, I got a call a little after midnight that my niece Delilah was on her way to get me. the news was going on with Momma. Delilah picked me and Kaleah up and we raced to my mom's apartment and I saw cops were there, but no ambulance. My stepsister Ivy was standing outside and I just knew. I think I knew the minute Delilah got to my house to get us: my momma had died. She was actually laying on the living room floor with a sheet covering her, her hand was sticking out from the sheet and I just laid down next to her and grabbed her hand. It was still warm and I could hold it and a part of me just died right there with her. What am I gonna do now? My momma was everything to me and my kids. Kaleah was with me but now we had to go wake up Kayden and Keannah and tell them that the person they loved the most in this world had died, and that hurt so bad.

I made all the calls and all the arrangements with Ivy and Papa at the funeral home, and took donations up there several times, and was beside myself with financial burden and stress. Me and Roci and Zachary and Papa managed to get her service taken care of and paid for, and my only concern was I wanted lots of flowers for Momma. She loved flowers and I wanted the place packed with them; I had given up that dream because the service took every penny we all had.

Momma's service was November 12, and it was in the air that Heather may or may not come, so I didn't know what to expect. In the back of my mind I could not imagine Heather not showing up at least to the funeral home. Out of nowhere, Heather showed up at my house in her SUV Zachary had got her and it was absolutely packed full of brand-new flowers!!! More flowers than I could ever dream of, and I just lost it. I played

Heather a song that I dedicated to Roci and Heather back in 2018 called "Somebody's Someone" by Daphne Willis, and I leaned down and hugged Heather so tight and told her I loved her and I missed her and I did not care about anything except us being sisters and I was so sorry for whatever I did that made her end our relationship. She told me she was sorry to and me, Heather and Roci. We each lit a joint for Momma and we celebrated our mom, the way she would have wanted us to.

Me and my sisters have never been closer and I truly cherish our bond that will last beyond this world.

Rest in peace Ms. Leah Abshire-Blevins. You can have all the flowers in heaven now.

I pray everyone finds peace in the pain and struggles of life. No matter how bad you have it, it can always be worse! Or it can get worse. I see now looking back that my life is that of a survivor, and though I did make some horrible decisions as a human and most regrettably as a mom, I am and always will be God's child, and he will always bring me through. I look forward to my next journey in this life after finding real peace in my whole heart, helping others not feel alone or afraid, because no matter what you got going on life can change in a split-second for the good or the bad. I myself have been both a monster and a hero to people depending on when they met me. To everyone I was a monster to, I do ask for forgiveness for my mistakes.

I was able to find real forgiveness for Tonio, for myself and truly hope that he can share his story and make something better and maybe change some lives with his testimony. Because to me, if I don't share my story, our story and try to let others know the warning signs and simply what not to put up with, regardless of love or whatever is keeping them in a bad situation, then what me and my family have gone through is for no reason. I would like something positive to come out of my life.

As all of the above played such a direct role in making me the survivor I am proud to be today, I am truly grateful. God saved me and my family.

I WANT EVERYONE TO SPEAK UP, SILENCE IN THESE MATTERS IS VIOLENCE

Written by Hannah Kendrick August of 2018

This came to me one day. God put it in my heart to share with all of you.

Once there was a girl born, but a child of no innocence at all. She had no clue she was in pain because her normal was so disturbing. Every day she just pushed through the pain. She went on the only way she could. She would soon learn her life was dark and very abnormal. She sought out happiness in a bottle only to find herself drowned in despair of emotions. She cried out loud. She screamed and yelled, "Dear God, take me out of hell." She hit her knees and in that moment the sun came from behind a cloud and her heavenly father said, "I'm here my dear child. I have been here the whole time. If you just call out for me, I will make you free from any needs. I declare there is nothing I can't walk or carry you through. My child, I know it's been hard. Read my words and just believe your sweet soul is mine forever, my child."

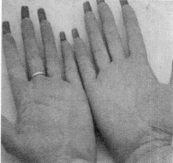

Made in the USA
Coppell, TX
03 August 2022